In Search
of the Cross

LeAnn Hartzler

Gazelle
PRESS

*Proceeds from the sale of this book
will be given to Pastor Tomas Bencomo to aid in his mission
to feed, clothe, educate and bring the light of the gospel
to the Tarahumara Indians.*

*For more information, please visit
www.insearchofthecross.com.*

Gazelle Press
P.O. Box 191540 • Mobile, AL 36619
800-367-8203

Dedication

I would like to dedicate this book to my family
who walked with me through the dark valley of the shadow of death
over those days when I was lost in the wilderness.

I dedicate it also to all those who were relentless in their search,
leaving no stone unturned in their efforts to find me, my teammates, Pastor
Tomas, all my friends at Rio Chico and many others who I've not had the
opportunity to thank. And finally to God, my ultimate rescuer!
To Him be all the glory!

Acknowledgments

Thanks to Becky Hussey for her help in getting this project off the ground and to Verna Clemmer for her editing and helpful suggestions. Thanks also to Pastor Jorn and Pastor Ron for their constant encouragement without which I may have easily given up. Thanks to Keith Carroll for coaching me in the publishing process and to Nathanael Waite for his expertise in developing the website. Thanks to my parents for their support and help in making this dream become a reality. Thanks also to my teammates who shared their hearts, their experiences and their photos, all pieces of the puzzle, which makes our story come alive.

Table of Contents

Preface

You are about to embark on a journey. We invite you to come with us on a missions trip to the Sierra Madre mountains of north central Mexico where we will be working alongside a pastor with a heart of compassion for a previously unknown people group called the Tarahumara. We will introduce you to Pastor Tomas Bencomo and the Indians he ministers to. You will also experience the camaraderie and laughter that happens when God handpicks this team of ten men and two women for the work that needs to be done. When the unexpected happens and one of the team goes missing, you will encounter the drama from the perspective of the lost as well as from the team leader in Mexico and folks back home.

In the midst of it all and in a myriad of ways, we will also experience the presence of God. His Word tells us that He will never leave us. Never, means never. So forever and always God is with us whether we recognize it or not. What is it about this missions experience in Mexico that makes God's presence seem so real, almost tangible? Is it because we begin and end each day with worship and the Word? God's Word says that He inhabits the praises of His people. We are led powerfully in worship each morning and evening, bringing us into the presence of God. We also spend time in the Word, allowing God to speak to our hearts corporately and individually.

We experience fellowship with likeminded brothers and sisters. God promises that where two or more are gathered in His name, there He will be in the midst of them. God's presence dwells in the hearts of those around us as we come together in unity of purpose to do all we can to assist Pastor Tomas with his ministry to the Indians. We are doing God's work, and He is at work among us. We allow ourselves to be thrust into situations that are beyond ourselves, where we are forced to rely on God and allow Him to work through us. When we reach the point of our limitation, He takes over and completes the work.

There is nothing in Rio Chico to distract us from what God had called us to do. No cell phones, no email, no radio or television. Our time is spent totally focused on God and what He is doing in us and through us. The cross that sits high on the cliff above camp is a constant reminder of "the Word becoming flesh and dwelling among us." Jesus' sacrifice on the cross and His shed blood sprinkled on heaven's mercy seat restores our relationship with the Father and provides the way for us to enter into His throne room, into the very presence of God.

Come along on our journey *In Search of the Cross* and discover the pathway to God's presence.

Chapter One

THE BEGINNING

by LeAnn

At 4:00 a.m. on February 4, 2006, I, along with a group of nine men and one other woman embarked on a journey. From the moment I decided to take the trip, I knew it would be a journey like no other journey I had ever experienced. We departed from the parking lot of Grace Covenant Church in Lewistown, Pennsylvania, in the church bus driven by Mr. Prendergast. Sam Boob, Tom Smith, Shawn McNeil, Davy Kerstetter, Ben Hartzler, Larry Shaffer Jr., Josh Neff, Denny and Diane Snook, Pastor Jorn Junod, and I were all excited about our mission trip and what God had in store for us during our ten days in Mexico, but we were oblivious to the test of faith that we would encounter while there.

Some fell asleep due to the early hour, but others of us were too excited to even consider closing our eyes for a nap. The wonder of what lay ahead for us in the coming days swirled through our minds and stirred our hearts. Pastor Michael Bailey and his wife, Jane, made the trip with us to the Baltimore airport. Pastor Michael founded Grace Covenant Church in response to a prompting of the Holy Spirit. He returned from Bible College in Florida to his home area of central Pennsylvania to begin a church there. Grace Covenant Church was established on September 17, 1988, beginning with family members and eventually growing and maturing into the vibrant church family that it is today.

Pastor Michael is not only a great preacher and teacher. He is also uniquely gifted as a mentor and spiritual father, raising up new leaders as his spiritual sons in the Lord. He has lovingly guided, directed, and nurtured them while imparting wisdom and providing a powerful example of excellent leadership. One of these leaders is Danny Neff who currently shepherds the people of Grace Covenant Church in Mount Union, Pennsylvania, a sister church to Grace Covenant Church in Lewistown. I met Danny years before when he was serving as a law enforcement officer in the small town where I live. It was not because I was breaking the law that I met Danny. He never pulled me over for speeding or anything like that, although he probably could have a time or two. Rather, I was blessed with an opportunity to meet him because he loved people. He took time to get to know and encourage the people he served. I have always enjoyed walking the back roads of "Big Valley," and when our paths crossed, he would often stop his patrol car along the side of the road to chat. He wanted to make sure I was not being harassed by anyone when I was walking alone on the secluded roads, but he also wanted to find out how my walk with the Lord was going. His genuine concern touched me deeply; so, when I was looking for a church in the spring of 1999, I decided to visit Grace Covenant Church where Danny was then serving as associate pastor.

There I discovered that Pastor Danny's heart mirrored that of his mentor, Pastor Michael. I immediately felt a connection to the church body. At the time, Pastor Michael was mentoring two other young men for leadership roles—Jorn Junod, who was serving as the youth pastor, and Ron Neff, Danny's brother. Ron later took Danny's place as associate pastor when Danny left to plant a new church in Mount Union, Pennsylvania, just up the road from Lewistown.

In November 2005, after much fasting and prayer, Pastor Michael decided it was time to take on a different role. Less than a week prior to our trip, he turned the reins of Grace Covenant Church in Lewistown over to his "sons in the Lord." Ron would serve as pastor and Jorn would assume the role of associate pastor, as well as continuing to oversee the youth ministry program. Pastor Michael remains an overseer of the church, but his mission now is to focus on raising up new church leaders. After more than eight years at Grace Covenant Church, I have come to love, admire, and respect each of these fine men of God very much. I believe God has uniquely positioned each of them not only in their work, but also for the events surrounding the story told in this book.

Shortly after I began attending Grace Covenant Church, Pastor Jorn's wife, Bonnie, invited me to visit their Life Group. Life Groups are formed to provide church members with an opportunity to interact with other Christians and to share life lessons with one another. The groups get together to laugh, cry, pray, study the Bible, or to simply love each other and enjoy one another's fellowship. For several years, I was a part of Bonnie and Jorn's small group. It was through this group that my faith life was nurtured and challenged. I will be forever grateful for Jorn and Bonnie's influence in my life. They've blessed me with love, encouragement and wise counsel over the years. Another way

Jorn influenced me was through his love for missions. He has such a passion for people that you are bound to catch a little of it just by being around him. There was a seed planted in my heart for missions work years ago, but Jorn watered the seed and caused it to grow. It was during the time when I was a part of their Life Group that Jorn was given the responsibility of developing a Missions Board for the church. He asked me to consider serving on the board. He told me he wanted me to be a part of that work and he wanted me to go on a mission trip, which would be a requirement for serving on the board.

Though I don't remember ever discussing it with Jorn, I already had a desire to go on a mission trip and had wanted to do so for a very long time. I have had opportunities on three occasions to visit the country of Argentina—twice to visit my brother who was living there while he was wooing the woman who would later become my sister-in-law and the last time to visit my friend Roberto and his family. I had never gone there as part of a mission's experience though. On the last trip several years ago, Roberto, his wife, Ceci, their two young sons, and I traveled from the Atlantic coast of Argentina to the Andes Mountains on its western border with Chile. During our cross-country trip, I spent a couple of nights with a family who had a guest room built onto the side of the house. The room was built with logs that did not fit together tightly, and it was infested with spiders. There were spider holes in what seemed like every nook and cranny between the logs. The first morning there, I found a particularly large one exploring my face after crawling out of the jacket I was holding. I, of course, screamed and was quite concerned about where the spider had gotten to, but Roberto prophetically quipped, "You are just being prepared for a mission trip." I could hardly go to sleep that night, thinking about sharing the room with those spiders. I knew they must have been on my bed the night before because that's where my coat had been when the spider evidently crawled into it. A bit wiser, the second morning, I decided to shake out my clothes before putting them on, and sure enough, a spider fell out of my sweatshirt and scurried across the bathroom floor.

That may have prepared me for the living conditions on a mission field, but when we got back to my friend's hometown, something else happened that prepared my heart for this mission trip. One afternoon I decided to go for a walk to the river, and on my way back, I was going through a very poor section of town. There I saw a baby lying on his belly in the dusty street outside a house, which was little more than a shack. The child was chewing on what looked like a piece of a belt that had fallen off a car engine. The scene pierced my heart. I wanted so badly to somehow make a difference in that baby's life and living conditions, yet I felt powerless and unprepared to do anything. I did not even feel I could pick him up to love and comfort him because I was afraid his mother would misunderstand my intent, and I was unable to speak enough of their language to explain my actions.

The image of this baby and the desire to make a difference was still very clear in my mind and on my heart when Jorn showed me pictures of his first trip to Mexico one evening before our life group meeting. After seeing the photos and hearing Jorn speak about his trip, I knew I wanted to go there one day. I may not be able to go back to Argentina to bless the helpless child I saw on the street, but I hoped that I could do something to touch the lives of Mexico's poor in the Copper Canyon.

Now here I was on my way to the airport in answer to the call that God had placed in my heart a long time ago. On our way through a construction zone in the Lewistown Narrows, Pastor Jorn asked if everyone had their passport or birth certificate. Denny Snook was very embarrassed as he raised his hand and said, "No, Pastor, I don't have mine." We made the first available U-turn and headed back to Lewistown to the Snook residence where Denny found his passport and raced back to the bus. Satisfied that everyone now had what was needed, we were once again on our way and had no further delays on our trip to the airport.

I don't think it was just coincidence that I came upon that baby lying in the street in Argentina those years earlier. Nothing else will stir a heart for missions more than seeing a child living in poverty. God was with me that day, guiding my footsteps, urging me in the required direction so as to encounter that scene. He's always guiding us, bringing experiences into our lives that are not only for today, but are also stepping stones into the future He has planned for us.

Chapter Two

WHY MEXICO?

by LeAnn

Pastor Jorn and others from our church had made two previous trips to Mexico to partner with Pastor Tomas Bencomo in his ministry to the Tarahumara Indians of the Copper Canyon. A number of years ago, Dave Aurand, a member of our church, went with a group from a local Christian and Missionary Alliance Church to help with the construction of the guest-house at Pastor Tomas' base camp at Rio Chico. When he returned, he spoke with Pastor Jorn about his experience and suggested we invite Pastor Tomas to come and speak to our church about his ministry.

Pastor Tomas, who lives in Juarez, Mexico, is affiliated with the Christian and Missionary Alliance Church. He has planted seventeen churches in and around the Juarez area and is currently pastoring a church he planted in El Paso, Texas. About fourteen years ago, Pastor Tomas was watching the news on television when he saw a report concerning the Tarahumara Indians. His heart was touched by the plight of these people that he never before knew existed. The Mexican government will help the Indians if they come out of the canyon, but because it is so difficult to reach them, little has been done to take help directly to them. Pastor Tomas felt called by God to do something to assist the Tarahumara. Since then, he has been working to locate and minister to the needs of these destitute people. In one area, Pastor Tomas is building a school and dormitory with the hope that children from across the canyon will come to the school to be educated and to be taught the Word of God. He also makes monthly trips from his base camp at Rio Chico into the canyon with food and clothing for the Indians. Others, including a man named Gonzalo, are helping with the monthly trips to the canyon so they can go into a number of different areas. Medical care is also desperately needed. Pastor Tomas works hard to find and bring in as much medical assistance as he can and sometimes takes teams of medical doctors to some of the more accessible areas so they can treat the Indians' physical needs. Part of the work he has done to help feed the people includes farming to raise food to take into the canyon. Horses or mules are needed to take provisions into the canyon, as motorized transportation is nearly impossible in the rugged terrain. Amish people from Central Pennsylvania have donated nine mules to Pastor Tomas to help with this vital need. It was a practical and much needed gift that was deeply appreciated.

The Tarahumara Indians were originally known as the Raramuri, which means running people. Spaniards coming into the area began calling these people the Tarahumara and were never corrected, so the name has remained to this day. The Tarahumara Indians are known as outstanding runners and living in high altitudes has caused them to develop amazing lung capacity. Stories have been told that, centuries ago, the men would hunt deer and mountain goats by chasing them until the animal fell from exhaustion. There are an estimated 20,000—50,000 Indians (some estimates run as high as 70,000) living in caves where their ancestors fled from slavery imposed on them by the Conquistadors. It is very rugged terrain. Most people would find it to be an inhospitable place; yet, the Indians are living there—deep in the canyons, in areas that are very hard to reach. There are no roads into the areas where the Indians live, so getting to them requires hiking the steep canyons and crossing rivers by precarious means, such as a cart suspended from a cable or a rope bridge high above the water. They live in simple huts or stone structures, often using cave walls or cliffs as part of their dwelling. Inside, there is generally little more than a cooking area made of stones. The floor is dirt, and the roof is made of sticks or branches. They are uneducated and live a very difficult life, with little to eat. Because they are so isolated and have no doubt passed on stories of their ancestor's slavery from generation to generation, the Indians are suspicious and are usually reluctant to associate with Pastor Tomas. It takes him nearly a year of providing gifts of food and clothing and showing them love to earn the trust of each family he finds. They live separate lives and do not typically form communities. This tendency to remain disconnected and isolated from each other adds to the difficulty in locating them. Because the land is dry, crops are difficult to cultivate and hunger is a major problem. The dwellings they have constructed for themselves simply do not provide enough shelter for surviving the sometimes bitter cold that comes to the high elevations. They also do not have sufficient clothing to keep themselves warm, and most of the children have never owned a pair of shoes. The life expectancy of the Tarahumara is a short forty-five years, but Pastor Tomas told me that fifty percent of the children die of starvation, disease, or exposure before reaching their tenth birthday.

Pastor Tomas goes into the canyon to minister to the Indians' physical needs, but his primary concern is a spiritual one. Most of the Indians have had no opportunity to hear the Gospel, and Pastor Tomas has seen evidence of demonic influence in the canyon. So, along with the food and clothing, Pastor Tomas and those helping him share the love of God and the salvation message with the Indians.

Pastor Tomas and the others working with him have heard the call of God to reach out and minister to the needs of the Tarahumara people. God is with us in the call He's placed in each of us to see through His eyes to the needs of those around us. He has a purpose for each of our lives, something for each of us to do. He has equipped each of us for our specific purpose and will be with us as we endeavor to fulfill His plans for our lives.

Chapter Three

WHY RIO CHICO?

by Pastor Jorn

When Pastor Tomas came to speak at our church, I (Jorn) knew that he was a spirit-filled Christian by the way he spoke of his ministry. When he showed us pictures of the Copper Canyon and his ministry to the Indians, I knew immediately that I wanted to go there. Photographs depicting the ride across the river at the bottom of the canyon stirred the adventurer in me. Pastor Tomas and the Indians built a wooden cart and hung it on a cable stretched across the river, high above the roaring water below. The cart is moved across the cable using a pulley system. In one direction, all that is required to move from one side of the river to the other is to release the rope holding the cart which leads to a ride nearly as thrilling as a rollercoaster at an amusement park. To move in the opposite direction, much more manpower is required. Some might find it a bit frightening, but to me it looked like great fun.

Seeing the pictures of his ministry to the Tarahumara people quickened another side of me—my love for people. My eyes were opened to the incredible need of these people living in the rugged canyon terrain. I shared with Michael my desire to go see Pastor Tomas' ministry for myself. We had been taking missions teams to Nicaragua, but that destination was no longer available to us. We were looking for somewhere else to take people from our congregation to serve God in short-term mission experiences and I thought this just might be the place. Pastor Michael agreed, and I invited Dave Aurand to go with me. On that trip, we saw every facet of Pastor Tomas' ministry: from the work he is doing in the city of Juarez, to the churches he has planted in the outlying areas. We saw the base camp at Rio Chico and the Copper Canyon where Pastor Tomas is building a school, a dormitory, and a home for a couple who has committed their lives to teaching the Indian children.

Although it was difficult, I really enjoyed hiking into the canyon. Dave and I quickly discovered that we were not as prepared for the arduous climb as we had thought. Aching muscles and blistering feet accompanied us on our hike. The Copper Canyon is the most magnificent place I have ever seen. The breathtaking views we encountered around every bend made every step worth the effort. As I was hiking the steep trails, I was considering who I could bring with me to this place. Who would have the kind of spirit it takes to make this very difficult trek into the canyon? I decided they would have to be risk takers, have the physical strength and stamina required to traverse the steep canyons, and have no fear of crossing the river. It was quite a long hike, so I had ample time to come up with a plan. I decided to first take a group of teens. If they made it into the canyon and back without too much trouble, I knew I would be able to take others to help with the work there as well.

Later that summer, I took a group of our teens to the canyon. Some of the teens stayed at a village on the rim of the canyon where they did children's ministry. The other teens hiked with me into the canyon to work on construction of the school. The work in the canyon moves very slowly due to lack of funds for building supplies and because all the supplies have to be brought in on the backs of the mules. When they have the money to buy supplies and the supplies have all been brought in, then all the work is done manually. The teens and I mixed cement by hand for the floor of one of the buildings and worked on digging the foundation for another out of the side of the mountain using picks and shovels. Except for some illness and sore muscles, the teens all survived their canyon experience, and I was already excitedly anticipating the next trip.

During our stay over at the base camp in Rio Chico, Pastor Tomas showed me around the camp. I quickly realized there were a lot of needs there as well. He showed me his fleet of pickup trucks that were badly in need of repair. The tires were bald, the brakes were nearly non-existent, and the gas lines had been rerouted to the bed of each pickup because they had only one container of gas and one battery that they moved from vehicle to vehicle, depending on which one they needed to use that day. They also had a lot of gas stolen out of the gas tanks, which was another reason for using one container that could be locked inside one of the buildings when not in use.

We walked over to the barn with its incomplete second story. I did not know how long the barn had remained unfinished, but this work also suffered from a lack of finances to buy the necessary building supplies. I noticed they also needed a few gates to control the movement of the livestock. As we walked around camp, I started making a list in my mind of all the things I wanted to do for them. I prayed, asking God who He wanted me to bring here, and I immediately began to see faces of people in our church who were gifted to fill the needs I had seen. I was thinking about the next trip to the canyon and wanted to bring people whose appetites might be whet for a future trip into the canyon after having been to Rio Chico. One of those people I wanted to bring and whom I knew we needed if we were to be successful was Davy Kerstetter. I knew he might be reluctant to come because he had never been away from his wife and children. God would have to intervene if he were to make the trip. There were people who told me there was no way Davy Kerstetter would go, but God is bigger than man's excuses!

My heart is always stirred by the needs of people. It's God that does that. He's with us when He fills our hearts with His passion to love people and care about their needs over our own. God could reach down and supernaturally provide for the needs of those around us, but most of the time He chooses to partner with us in meeting those needs.

Chapter Four

WHY ME?

by LeAnn

After that trip to Rio Chico, Pastor Jorn met with our Mission's Board and described to us what he had seen there and explained the needs to us. He told the board about the vehicles that needed a lot of repairs and described the unfinished second story of the barn. If the vehicles could be repaired, Pastor Tomas would have much more reliable transportation. Completion of all this work would equip him for his outreach to the Indians, which was of more concern to him than his needs. Pastor Jorn told us that as he looked at the needs, in his mind, he began to picture faces of people gifted in the type of work that was needed. He gave us a list of the names of the people he wanted to go on the next trip and asked us to pray over those names. I was thrilled and excited to be one of the people he mentioned that day. Every single person whose name was on that list had gotten on the bus with me that morning, even Davy. God had handpicked this team and brought us together. Many of us did not know one another well, yet He blended us together in love and for His purpose.

Tom Smith said after seeing the video from Jorn and Dave Aurand's trip, he sensed he would be going to Rio Chico one day. When Jorn came to him and said, "You are going with me to Rio Chico," he readily accepted Jorn's somewhat forceful invitation. Jorn didn't need to twist his arm though. He had already decided he wanted to go, even prior to being asked. Davy, on the other hand, was a bit more reluctant. When Jorn talked to him about going, he asked if he could think and pray about it for a while, but in the back of his mind he was thinking he'd be able to come up with some excuse not to go. He thought his employer or his wife might tell him they didn't want him to go, but God had other plans. He showed Davy the scripture passage from Luke 10:2 that says, "The harvest is plentiful, but the workers are few" (NIV). God spoke to his heart, delivered him from fear, and convinced him this trip to Rio Chico was part of His plan for Davy's life. Denny and Diane had heard Pastor Tomas speak at church. With each of their jobs to consider, it was not easy to get their schedules to mesh, but they managed to do it. God had caused everything to fall into place so they could go. Larry Shaffer, Jr. felt the gentle push of the Holy Spirit prompting him after hearing Pastor Tomas speak and seeing the video of Jorn and Dave's trip. He saw the need and was delighted to have the opportunity to go and do what he could to help. Sam had been to Haiti on a mission trip and didn't really want to go to Mexico at first. But he saw that the Lord had brought the group together and felt a stirring in his heart. He wanted to go and to serve as well.

I had missed both of those opportunities to hear about Pastor Tomas' work in Mexico. When he came to speak at our church, I was working late in Lancaster County. I was sick and not able to be at church the morning Jorn and Dave shared. But it was clear to me through the pictures Jorn showed me later, and the information he shared with all of us that there was a need, a great need, for us to reach out. We all wanted to help Pastor Tomas serve the needs of the Tarahumara Indians. We all knew that the work we would be doing in Mexico would help Pastor Tomas fulfill his mission, and we were thrilled to be a part of it.

In a meeting back in January, Pastor Jorn told us he would be fasting and praying in the weeks leading up to our trip, and he encouraged all of us to be in prayer as well. I was already fasting and praying daily for a friend who had recently been diagnosed with stage-four cancer, but not a full fast like Jorn was. I decided to include our trip in my fast and began also to pray for each of the team members and for Pastor Tomas and his ministry. I asked God to use this experience to bring all of us closer to Him and to each other as He used us in whatever way He chose. I desperately wanted to be used by God and to have my heart changed. I wanted this experience to be life changing. I wanted my heart to be turned away from myself to the needs of others. I wanted to come back deeper in love with Jesus and more like Him in every way.

I had grown up in the church. My parents took me to church from the time I was born and I'm very grateful for that. But, because of that, I didn't have a drastic life change when I accepted Jesus as my Savior as a pre-teen. I didn't have a dramatic salvation experience or testimony. I knew when we returned from Mexico Pastor Jorn was going to expect us to have something to share with the church, so I prayed that I would come home with a testimony. Had I only known!

God speaks to each of us uniquely and individually. Each of us heard His voice and His call to go to Mexico. We all knew we had heard His voice and were expecting Him to use us for His glory. He didn't call us together only to send us on our merry way. He was one of us and was going along with us. I think He was probably as excited as we were about what was ahead and like us, He wouldn't have wanted to miss it for the world.

Chapter Five

THE FUN STARTS

by LeAnn

Now, as our bus approached the airport, the image of that poor baby lying on its belly in the dusty street in Argentina was not far from my thoughts, only now I did not have a sense of being powerless. Not only was a part of a skilled team, but also our church family had given generously, so we would have the funds we needed to purchase any necessary tools, truck parts, and building supplies. We were also equipped with the love of God and the power of the Holy Spirit to do something special to touch the lives of Mexico's poor in the Copper Canyon.

At the airport, we were dropped off at the curb. We unloaded our massive amount of luggage and made our way to the check-in line. When we were all checked in, we headed to the gate. We passed Pastor Michael and Jane who had time for breakfast before their flight to Texas, where they were spending the week at a Ministers' Conference. We, on the other hand, arrived at the gate just four minutes before its closing. Our breakfast would have to wait until we reached Minneapolis!

It was Davy and Larry's first flight. Davy sat next to me and asked several times if certain bumps and noises were normal. I assured him they were. Larry though, who suffers from vertigo, was too sick to care. In a conversation with God, he said, "Lord, this had better be worth it," and a little later a team member slapped him on the back and said, "Don't worry, brother, it's going to be worth it," but I don't think he was convinced just yet. He said he just wanted someone to put a gun to his head and put him out of his misery. It was that bad!

At our stopover in Minneapolis, most of us used the moving sidewalks to get around the airport, but not Larry. He was still feeling woozy and had had enough of unnatural motion. He chose to navigate areas that did not move under his feet and refused to even glance over at the rest of us as we were sailing by him.

The second flight went smoothly, and Larry didn't get quite as sick this time. Finally on the ground in El Paso, we were excited to catch up with Kevin Snyder in the airport. Kevin and his family are members of our church who, at the time, were in full-time ministry with Mercy Ships, a world-class missions operation that serves the needs of people all around the world. He was going along to help with the work and to explore the possibility of Mercy Ships one day also sending teams to help Pastor Tomas in his ministry.

Outside, we met Pastor Tomas and his assistant, Brenda Granados, for the first time. While Pastor Tomas does speak some English, he often calls upon Brenda to serve as his interpreter. Brenda is a wonderful woman who has spent the last fifteen years working alongside Pastor Tomas. She works very hard and willingly does whatever is required of her. She manages the finances, cares for the groups that visit, and even hikes into the canyon with Pastor Tomas. She organized everything for us from our meals to our transportation and lodging. She had it all covered. Some referred to her as "wonder woman" as she maneuvered our van over the rough back streets of Juarez! We all felt honored to have an opportunity to work alongside these wonderful, gifted people of God.

The men had to bring all their tools with them, which was why we had a tremendous amount of luggage. It seemed unlikely that it would all fit in the back of the truck that was brought to transport it, but Pastor Tomas, who obviously had done this before, managed to stow it all safely. He seemed to know just how to make it all fit. We piled into the van and drove off toward the Mexican border. We were taken to the Bible Institute in Juarez, Mexico, where we would spend the night. The Bible Institute seemed quite luxurious compared to the living conditions of those living outside its walls. As we stood on the upstairs balcony, we could see homes all around the compound, some having walls made of cardboard or assorted scraps of lumber. These dwellings sit very close to their neighbor's home and right next to the dusty streets. We saw very few children, as there is no place for them to play outside their homes. There is a soccer field behind the Institute, but we only saw a couple of children there.

Three little girls were spending the afternoon at the Institute that day. We had a great

Our playmates

time playing soccer, tag, and hide-n-seek with them, after figuring out what it was they wanted to do. That was a challenge since they spoke no English and we spoke little Spanish. It was a lot of fun, but they soon wore all of us out. Even without travel fatigue to slow us down, I don't think we could have matched the youthful energy of the girls. Davy asked me how to say, "Where is your mother?" in Spanish. Then, he stood at the top of the wall with one hand on his hip and the other in the air and loudly questioned, "Donde esta you mama?" just as their mothers appeared around the side of the building. That was just the beginning of the side-splitting laughter we would experience throughout the week.

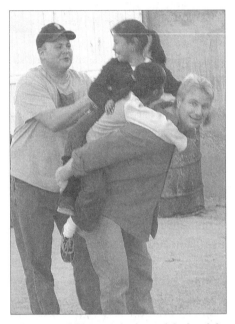

Davy and Shawn playing with the girls

Later, we all went out to dinner at a nice restaurant with Brenda, Pastor Tomas, and his wife, Maria. And we were at it again, laughing so hard that we had the attention of everyone in the place. Pastor Tomas and Brenda were sitting at one end of the table and were watching the rest of us laughing with Larry who was gnawing on a particularly tough steak. Thankfully he was finally over his sickness and had his appetite back. Pastor Jorn leaned over toward Pastor Tomas, so he could be heard over the noise we were making, and said, "Brother, it's going to be like this for the next ten days, so you might as well get used to it!" He was right. Later, twenty hours after my day had begun, I wrote in my journal, "I think I can honestly say I have never laughed so much in my life. What a group of live wires. It's going to be a fun week!"

In the presence of God, there is fullness of joy. Larry said it well when he said, "When you are doing something for God, He just makes it fun." And He did. He had brought together this rag tag bunch and filled us with joy in being together and doing His work.

Chapter Six

WORSHIP IN JUAREZ

by LeAnn

The next morning, as I was waking up, I was remembering the noises I had heard during the night, noises associated with both the city and the country. Along with the traffic noise and sirens, I had heard the sounds of dogs barking and roosters crowing. And that morning, there was a pigeon cooing somewhere in the ceiling. As I lay in my bed, I heard Jorn ask over the wall that didn't quite reach the ceiling, "How are you doing over there, LeAnn?" Something was stirring up my allergies and I was sniffing. I think Jorn must have thought I was crying, but I was far from it. I was nearly giddy with excitement! I told him I never knew going on a mission trip would be so much fun, and I could not wait to get going!

I wrote in my journal, "I am really looking forward to what God has in store for us this week. I don't want to miss any opportunity to bless Pastor Tomas and his ministry in Rio Chico and the canyon. Lord, we want to hear your voice this week; to draw near to you, to lift you up, and to be ministers of your grace."

A very important part of our week together was the time we spent in worship and prayer, both individually and corporately. Each morning, Josh or Shawn would lead worship, and then someone from the team was assigned to reflect on scripture passages and share thoughts and insights with the rest of the group. And each evening we would again gather for worship, and Jorn would teach us from the Word. These were special times of fellowship and the lessons learned would all be lived out at some point during the week. During devotions, on this particular morning, Jorn told the group how he had prayed with the Mission's Board and had chosen a list of persons to come with him on this trip and that everyone on the list was there. God had definitely had a hand in putting our group together, which is further evidence of His sense of humor. He not only had our skills in mind when He chose us, but I think He fully understood the merriment that would happen when this particular group of

17

people was brought together. He also knew what we could accomplish when we were joined in purpose and how the group would pull together when faced with a crisis.

Jorn also talked to us that morning about how mission trips change lives. We would not be the same at the end of our experience in Rio Chico. He also told us people should be our most important priority during our time there and that we should take every opportunity to touch the lives of those we meet, so they might see a reflection of Jesus in us. Then Kevin led our devotional time and shared from the scripture passage found in the book of John 15:12, "Greater love has no one than this, that he lay down his life for his friends" (NIV). Kevin said we had done that by leaving our families and lives behind for those ten days.

Jorn said we all have needs, but God's Word says, "We have not, because we ask not." He told us God would honor our sacrifice. He encouraged us to search our hearts for the things we want from God and ask Him for them, reminding Him of what we were doing for Him this week. He also told us to be motivated by love and not by fear. The reason for our being there and for everything we do is our love for God and for those we were there to serve.

Because of my previous travel to Argentina, I was familiar with the upbeat tempo of Spanish worship and could hardly wait to get to church to experience the joyful Latin rhythms again. I was not disappointed at Iglesia Encuentro Con Dios which, when translated into English, means, "Encounter with God Church." The church building itself was simple, with the capacity to seat, perhaps, one hundred people. What made the church so special was not only the wonderful band but also the exuberant praise filling the room and warming our hearts. After the singing, Pastor Jorn preached, while Brenda translated. His text was Ephesians 3:14-19.

> *My response is to get down on my knees before the Father, this magnificent Father who parcels out all heaven and earth. I ask Him to strengthen you by His Spirit—not a brute strength, but a glorious inner strength—that Christ will live in you as you open the door and invite Him in. And I ask Him that with both feet planted firmly on love, you'll be able to take in, with all Christians, the extravagant dimensions of Christ's love. Reach out and experience the breadth! Test its length! Plumb the depths! Rise to the heights! Live full lives, full in the fullness of God.*

He spoke to us about God's concept of family and how the example of our individual families needs to be incorporated into the church. Psalm 68:6 states that God sets the lonely in families. He told us that sometimes it is easy to allow some people into the church, but it is far more difficult to allow them into our hearts. The only way God can set the lonely in families is through us. We need to have the eyes of our hearts focused on what God sees as important and accept those who might appear unlovely.

God is three in one because He represents family. Sometimes, we need a father, God, to give us guidance. Sometimes we need a brother, Jesus, to come alongside and be our friend. Sometimes we need a comforter, the Holy Spirit, to soothe our pain like our mothers did when we were children. Every part of family is wrapped up in God, but we also need the church to be family. James 1:27 says, "Pure religion, the kind that passes muster before God the Father, is this: Reach out to the homeless and loveless in their plight, and guard against corruption from the godless world." We won't stand before God with a list of things we've done, but with a list of people whose lives we've touched. There is a part of God we miss when we refuse to leave our comfort zones and reach out to those who need the love of a family.

Hebrews 12:2 says,

Keep your eyes on Jesus, who both began and finished this race we are in. Study how He did it. Because He never lost sight of where He was headed—that exhilarating finish in and with God—He could put up with anything along the way, cross, shame, whatever. And now He's there, in the place of honor, right alongside God.

We need to see through the eyes of God to the hearts of those around us and not lose sight of the goal, living lives that touch others with the love of God.

It was a powerful sermon and the Holy Spirit was at work in the hearts of those in attendance. Many went forward for ministry. We also shared a very special time of communion with the church, each of us receiving the elements of communion as the bread and the wine were passed among us. The presence of God was evident as we followed Jesus' command to "do this in remembrance of me." We felt a special bond with the Mexican people as we sang the song, "The Old Rugged Cross." Our voices combined—our languages melded. It did not matter that the local people were singing in Spanish, and our team was singing in English. The presence of God tore down any of the cultural barriers between us, and we were one in Christ, all part of the family of God. He moved among us that morning and joined our hearts together in love as brothers and sisters, remembering what Christ has done to restore our relationship with the Father we all share.

Chapter Seven

ON THE ROAD

by LeAnn

After lunch, we packed up the truck again, piled into the van, and headed out of Juarez toward Rio Chico. Following behind was Pastor Tomas in the truck carrying our luggage and a car occupied by Gabriel and Christian, young men Pastor Tomas had hired to help us with our work in Rio Chico. It's generally a six to eight hour drive. The travel time is estimated in broad terms because one never knows just how long it might take. Time management is not something that holds a high priority in Hispanic cultures. The trip could be elongated due to an unplanned stop to visit someone or simply because it is time for siesta, but nothing is ever hurried in Mexico. Whenever our patience wore thin, Jorn with an understanding grin would remind us that we were in Mexico.

Again, the van was filled with laughter, which made the ride seem not so long. On our way across the border into Chihuahua, we were stopped and asked to show our passports and to tell the official we were Americans. He checked under and around the van, then, before waving us off, he looked in the window, grinned, and said, "Seattle is going to win!" (You see, it was Super Bowl Sunday and we had taken our Super Bowl party on the road. Little did our grinning, border patrolman know that Jorn had borrowed a satellite radio so we could listen to the Super Bowl game on the way to Rio Chico, but he must have noticed the Steelers garb worn by some of our football fans.) Laughter erupted again which helped to alleviate the anxiety over yet another border crossing. Later, the guys were sure it was a gift from the Lord when they were able to catch the first touchdown on the television behind the counter at a little store where we stopped for a snack and a bathroom break. I wondered what the locals behind the counter were thinking as they watched all these gringos standing there with their eyes glued to the television above their heads.

We had gotten separated from Pastor Tomas' pickup and the car that

Christian and Gabriel were driving, when the car sprung a leak in the radiator. Fortunately we had a couple of knowledgeable mechanics with us who assessed the situation and suggested they add water to the radiator before going any further. We left them behind to take care of the car and went on our way.

A little later, we came upon a military checkpoint and were waved though, but when Pastor Tomas got there, he was stopped and the vehicle searched. The authorities wanted to know why Pastor Tomas was alone with so many pieces of luggage, all of which had to be unloaded so the guards could go through it. They also questioned his need for so many tools and suspected he was taking them into the next state to sell them. He called us and asked us to stop where we were because he thought the officials might require us to return to the checkpoint to claim our luggage. We prayed for favor as we parked along the side of the road, and Pastor Tomas called again a few minutes later to tell us they were allowing him through. This was just the first of many miracles we would be a part of on this trip, but then Larry might think his surviving the flight was the first.

Pastor Tomas, Christian, and Gabriel caught up with us when we stopped for dinner. Some of our group were reluctant to go into the restaurant and chose to stay behind in the van until the end of the football game. Most of us used a finger pointing method for ordering from the menu, and some were more adventurous than others. Diane, for example, ordered seafood soup, which included octopus tentacles complete with suction cups, while others had good old-fashioned American hamburgers. Some said, "It's better than the steak we had last night!" That was a comment we heard numerous times throughout the week. Others later wished they had stayed away from the chicken burritos.

Already, we were all beginning to sense unity within our group. There was no sense of self in this gathering. Everyone came together to be used in whatever capacity we were called.

A sixteen-hour drive separates Juarez, where Pastor Tomas lives, and the Copper Canyon where the Tarahumara live. So a number of years ago, a woman donated some land in the area known as Rio Chico, which is about half way between the two locations. Pastor Tomas built his base camp on this land, and this is where we would spend our week.

It was late and we were all ready for bed when we finally reached Rio Chico. We were again pleasantly surprised at how nice our accommodations were. Remembering my Argentina experience, I was expecting to have to check my shoes for spiders and scorpions before putting them on, but we

Home away from home

found it was not at all like that. The guesthouse was of good construction, carrying beauty in its simplicity. The windows were tight fitting and provided a barrier to the cold air outside, as well as any undesirable creatures that might have been lurking on the other side. The architecture bore a distinctive Spanish influence with arched entryways. Bright yellow exterior paint was highlighted with orange trim. Diane and I were assigned to one of the bedrooms which had its own bathroom with running water and a toilet that worked. Not everyone was so fortunate. We appreciated the running water despite the fact that sometimes it was cold water that came from the showerhead. Otherwise, it was like being at home. Well, except maybe for the lack of heat. The only source of heat in the building was a fireplace in the dining room, but our beds each had three wonderfully warm Indian blankets on them to comfort us.

God reminds us that He's with us when He hears and answers our prayers like He did when we asked for favor for Pastor Tomas at the military checkpoint. We would cry out to Him many times during the week and that reminder of His presence with us was something we would desperately cling to at the end of the week when we faced a crisis bigger than anything we could handle on our own.

Chapter 8

OUR HOME FOR SEVEN DAYS

by LeAnn

On the morning of the third day, we got our first glimpse of the surroundings at Rio Chico because we had arrived the night before under the cover of darkness. It truly is a magnificent place with mountain peaks and cliffs on every side. Dominating the landscape is a cross, made of steel beams, high on a cliff that overlooks the barn. The cross can be seen from anywhere around the camp. We would all, at some point during the week, make our way up to it, and it would play a significant role in our time at Rio Chico.

Cliff above the barn where the cross stands

The compound is made up of the guesthouse with two attached dwellings, the barn, two other one family dwellings, and assorted sheds. The buildings are situated between three mountains, and there is a creek that runs between the house and the barn.

Pastor Tomas' brother, Juan Bencomo, lives in this compound and serves as overseer of the base camp. Ivan and Francisco, also known as Chico, live there as well and assist with the work of the farm. Chico is a young man who was brought out of the canyon as a young boy, and since then, has been under Pastor Tomas' care. Ramon, who lives a short distance from the camp, helps with the horses and the general needs of the camp. He has two sons, Gilberto, a teenager, and Luis, who is ten years old, both boys enjoying helping out around the camp as well.

Two years ago, Pastor Tomas brought Rosenda and her two children, a four-year-old son, Lazaro, and a two-year-old daughter, Chabela, to live at Rio Chico. At the time, Rosenda and her children were living in a village called Pamache where Pastor Tomas had taken a group of doctors to treat the Indians' medical needs. Her husband had left her and the children two years earlier to work in another area and never returned. He left Rosenda and the children behind to live with his parents who did not treat her well, nor did they give her sufficient food for herself or the children. Lazaro was very ill, and in desperation, Rosenda asked Pastor Tomas for help. It was not known what was causing Lazaro's health issues, and Rosenda had no money for medical help or medications so Pastor Tomas brought her and the children out of the canyon to live at Rio Chico. Lazaro is now in good health and enjoys playing around camp with his little sister. Rosenda helps with the cooking and cleaning in the guesthouse and also cares for the smaller animals on the farm. The other two homes at the compound are occupied by families who Pastor Tomas says come and go, but we did not meet them during our time in Rio Chico.

That morning we discovered another of Brenda's wonderful gifts. In addition to her organizational skills and her ability to drive through the crowded rough streets of Juarez, she's also great cook. We all enjoyed and looked forward to the wonderful meals she and Rosenda cooked up for us. There were no complaints, only rave reviews concerning the food served at Brenda's table!

After a delightful breakfast, Shawn led our devotions. He talked to us about having a servant's heart. Galatians 6:9 says, "So let's not allow ourselves to get fatigued by doing good. At the right time, we will harvest a good crop if we don't give up or quit." He challenged us to consider what God might want to do in our hearts and told us that hardened hearts cannot be effective in ministry. Our hearts need to be pliable in the hands of the Father so He can shape them into hearts that will overflow with the love of Jesus.

Given my love for the outdoors and for walking, I could not resist a quick walk outside to take a few pictures and to check out the work to be done over at the barn before getting to my own assigned task. On my way there, I ran into a little boy playing with an old truck tire. I realized this must be Lazaro, Rosenda's son, and I couldn't wait for the opportunity to exchange that old tire for the soccer ball I had brought for him. Everyone was given jobs to do, and we all eagerly poured ourselves into our work. We were overwhelmed with the enormity of what needed to be done. From the huge pile of hay that needed to be moved in the barn so they could put a floor down, to the nearly hopeless task of making the vehicles run, to the paint rollers that refused to stay together, we were challenged many times in just our first day. We had to go back to Shawn's words from morning devotions many times. Shawn, though, spent most of that day sick in bed, being one of those who had consumed a chicken burrito the night before.

Denny, Diane, and I were given the task of painting the upstairs of the guesthouse where we were staying. When Diane and I got back from our tour of the barn, we found Denny already hard at work. There are seven bedrooms, five bathrooms, and a large meeting room on the second floor of the guesthouse; and they all needed a second coat of paint. To accomplish this task, we had to move all the things we had

Shawn fully recovered from his bout with the burrito

brought with us, as well as the beds we were using, in order to get to the walls and ceilings. It was quite challenging at times. At the end of the day, we had completed one bedroom and bath combination and had started on another, but we had also taken time out to play with the children and to bless them with gifts.

Rosenda's two children, Chabela and Lazaro, and Ramon's son, Luis, were a joy to have around. At first, the children were shy, but that quickly wore off and they were never very far away. They often skipped school and sometimes the bus just didn't show up, but either way, they were happy to spend the day with us.

The tasks assigned to us were sometimes overwhelming, more than what we could imagine ourselves capable of. In Matthew 14 Jesus told the disciples to feed the five thousand, definitely something they couldn't do on their own. Jesus could have told the people to sit down and then dropped food into their laps like manna from heaven, but He didn't do that. He chose to work through His disciples. But He didn't assign them the task and leave them to do it on their own. He worked alongside them and provided what they needed to get the job done. He's still doing that. He works with and through us to do more than we could do on our own. It's what He did in Rio Chico. We experienced His presence and His power at work in and through us to accomplish what otherwise seemed impossible.

Brothers Bencomo, Tomas & Juan

Brenda, aka "Superwoman"

Ramon & son, Luis

Rosenda's family & me

Shawn & children

Chapter Nine

WORK BEGINS

by Pastor Jorn

I (Jorn) spent that first morning at Rio Chico getting everyone started on the tasks assigned to them. We would be putting a floor down on the second story of the barn and laying adobe bricks to fill gaps in the walls where they had never been completed. The only way to reach the second story was by climbing a ladder leaning against the side of the building, so we would also complete the steps that had been started but stood unfinished. We would also be building several gates to close passageways in the stone walls that were constructed as fences for containing the animals.

Pastor Tomas and I talked every day during the week. Tomas is a quiet, humble man. His strength is based out of consistency. His emotions are not up and down. Because of that, I had confidence that when I went to him, I would always get the same kind of response. He has a conservative approach toward people who come there to help him, especially those he does not know well. When you get to know him, though, you find he really enjoys life. He is full of life, laughter, and joy. He has a wonderful sense of humor.

My interaction with Pastor Tomas during the week was always very positive. He and Brenda loved our group. He was so happy we were there and very grateful for the work we were doing. He was always thanking me for coming to help them. He did not tell me what to do and never looked over my shoulder. He just showed me the needs and left us to do what needed to be done. He released the work to us and trusted God that we would do it correctly. I can say with pride that wherever we've gone, we have always impacted the people we've served and the people we were with, in a very positive and life giving way. It doesn't matter if we're in Mexico, Nicaragua, or Nigeria, they always say, "Jorn, the people you brought with you are incredible! They have worked so hard and served with such a good attitude." And this trip was no exception. I was blessed daily by the attitude of those with me at Rio Chico and by what they were able to accomplish.

My responsibility was not necessarily to do the work, although I did do my share, but it was to be in constant contact with the people I had brought with me. My role was to encourage them, to be a source of strength and to tell them, "Hey, you're doing a great job!" I always made sure I was connecting with all of my people every day while the work was going on. Under normal circumstances, some might think I was just checking up on them and making sure they were getting something done. But that was never the real reason why I would stop by the guesthouse to watch the painters or walk over to see what the mechanics were doing. It was just so I could be in contact with them on a regular basis, to let them know I was thinking about them, to tell them I loved them, and to show my gratitude for their being there, serving God alongside me.

> **Davy** – "On the first day there, Sam and I looked over all the vehicles. The trucks were in terrible shape and when we looked under the hoods of some of them, we discovered that half the parts were missing. We didn't take a break until lunchtime and by then I was very overwhelmed by the work ahead of us. During our lunch break, I had a chance to take a few minutes to gaze at the mountains and the cross up on the cliff. As I took in the beauty of that place, a peace began to settle over my spirit and I went back to work with an assurance that with God's help, we could do the work required of us."

Many of the team members had never been on a mission trip before. Some had never been out of the United States. I had those thoughts in mind when I went on a twenty-nine day fast in January. I ingested just water and clear juices for twenty-nine days. I spent a lot of time in prayer concerning the trip. I prayed for those who were coming with me and for the relationships that I would be building with those whom I did not already have a strong relationship. I knew there is always a danger of relational struggles when you put a group together like this, especially since many of them did not know each other well prior to the trip. I went on the fast to prepare myself for whatever might come up. I knew I would need to be sensitive to how my people were feeling, how they were dealing with the culture shock, and any other struggles they might be having. So, it was very important that I made my rounds of the different work areas each day.

That first morning the Mexicans towed the trucks out into the middle of the yard where Davy and Sam could work on them. They had decided to go over the vehicles as they would for Pennsylvania inspections and began to list everything each vehicle needed. At the end of the row they came across a particularly hard case, a

Mechanics' challenge

nasty yellow pickup truck. A little later, I walked down to see how their work was going. As soon as I arrived, Davy started in on me about that yellow pickup truck. The famous saying of the week was: "Hey, let me tell you what!" and Davy said, "Hey, let me tell you what! You see that yellow truck over there? Well, you can just forget it. I'm not touching that thing. You just may as well tow that thing back there. I'm not even using it." Of course he thought I lied to him and wasn't honest about how bad the trucks were because I needed to get him down there. But if I lied, Lord, I didn't mean it, and I didn't do it on pur-

Hey, let me tell you what!

pose. But, you know God uses everything, doesn't He?

Later that evening, when we were sitting around the dinner table, Davy started in on me again. He said, "Hey, let me tell you what! I've never seen anything like this in my life!" And he started going on about that yellow truck again. I said, "Hey, let me tell you something. There was an older lady that used

31

to come to our church. Her name was Dorothy Leach. One day her car broke down, and it wouldn't work. So she laid her hands on her car and prayed. When she was through praying, the car was healed, and it started to work again!" Davy said, "Huh, let me tell you what!" He said, "Maybe you should have brought Dorothy Leach on this mission trip!" He told me "what" and everyone in the room broke out in fits of laughter! That's how every night was—every evening was filled with laughter. I laughed so hard, for so long, for so many nights that my gut hurt. I needed a break! We were literally laughing all the time.

God was not only with us as we worked, but He was with us during the fun fellowship times as well. He was filling us with joy and fulfillment at the end of each day's work.

Chapter Ten

TEAM'S TRADEMARK

by LeAnn

Stories abounded that evening at dinner when we all gathered, tired but filled with joy over what we had accomplished in just the first day. We all were enjoying each other so much and had such a good time working together. Our dinner conversations were always filled with laugher and those at Rio Chico enjoyed our laughter as well. They couldn't really understand what we were laughing about, but our laughter was infectious and transcended the language barrier.

That first night, the barn crew told us about the rats they encountered when they were moving the hay so they could put the new floor down. When they began to move the hay bales, rats came at them from all directions. They said the deeper they got into the stack of hay, the bigger the rats got. One of the guys joked that he thought he had seen a particularly large one with a pig in its mouth! They were all talking at once as they described to the rest of us the means they used to kill the rats. It was impossible to kill them all, there were just too many, but they did manage to kill some of them by stomping on them or stabbing them with pitchforks and shovels. They collected eight or ten of them and put them on top of the ladder that was leaning against the barn. Then they called Jorn over, knowing he'd have to climb the ladder to reach them. They said Jorn nearly fell off the ladder when he came face to face with the rats. He may have thought those laughing at him were the "rats," but he was a good sport about it and helped them finish moving the hay.

That evening after worship, Jorn talked to us about fear and asked us what our fears were concerning this trip. Romans 8:15 says, "This resurrection life you received from God is not a timid, grave-tending life. It's adventurously expectant, greeting God with a childlike, "What's next, Papa?" He said fear can become a taskmaster if not dealt with and can cause us to miss God. Fear works against faith and is the opposite of faith. Fear and faith cannot coexist.

Second Timothy 1:7 says, "For God has not given us a spirit of timidity, but of power, of love and of self-discipline" (NIV). The only way we can over-come fear is to face it, asking God to give us the power we need to overcome it. The proof that we love God is to live by faith. Psalm 34:4 says, "I sought the Lord and He answered me; He delivered me from all my fears" (NIV). First John 4:18 says, "There is no fear in love, but perfect love drives out all fear" (NIV). Love overcomes fear because it is connected to God. God's love and fear have nothing in common.

No one shared any fears that evening. We took in the lesson, though, and stored it away. It would become important later on in the week as many of the lessons brought forth in our devotional time would.

Laughter was indeed our team's trademark, and it connected us like nothing else could except maybe adversity, but that would come later. God is with us in the good and bad times. He created us to laugh and because we were created in His image, I believe He was laughing along with us.

Chapter Eleven

CONVERSATIONS WITH GOD

by LeAnn

On the morning of day four I got up early, took my Bible and journal and walked back along the creek that ran next to the house. It was another beautiful morning, and after a while, I sat down on a rock. I could no longer see the house from where I was, but I could still see the cross on the cliff above the barn, although just barely. God's presence felt so close as I read from the Psalms. As I sat there next to the river, gazing at the mountains, I was connecting with David in his wonder of God and His creation. I was overwhelmed with gratitude for the opportunity to be there and to serve God along with Pastor Tomas in his ministry to the Tarahumara Indians. Out of that sense of awe, wonder, and gratefulness, I wrote this prayer in my journal.

I'm overwhelmed and struggle to put into words all I feel about being here. Our work did not start off well yesterday and I believe the enemy was attempting to discourage us, but we pressed through and I sense that You are pleased with our offering. You, God, are the reason we are here. It's You who put love in our hearts for these people. Lord, it breaks my heart to see the conditions those around us are living in. They have so little and yet they joyfully share what they have with us because of You. Do your work in my heart this week. Turn my focus from myself to the needs of others. Search my heart with me and show me those areas that need to be surrendered to you and changed for your glory. Everything Lord, my life, all that I am and all that I have is Yours. Take it and use it for Your honor and glory. Make my life a sacrifice that is wholly pleasing to you.

Somehow I believe God said, "Alright, I'll do that."

When I got back to the house, we had breakfast and then it was Diane's turn to lead our daily devotions. She read the scripture passage from Philippians 2:1.

If you've gotten anything at all out of following Christ, if His love has made any difference in your life, if being in a community of the Spirit means anything to you, if you have a heart, if you care—then do me a favor. Agree with each other; love each other, be deep spirited friends.

Our unity on display

Diane then spoke of the importance of unity in the Spirit. She felt there was some significance in the fact that there were twelve of us, and Jesus had twelve disciples. She said she's awed by what Pastor Tomas and the others have accomplished here and can do here in the future, but it is all because of God's grace. She said that in our relationships as a group and with those around us, we need to find our common denominator, which is God's love. She shared with us her deep appreciation for the expression of unity during the communion service on Sunday when the local people sang in Spanish, and we sang along in English. God's presence in that place had erased any distinction that would set us apart from one another, and we were of one Spirit.

That morning Josh and Tom were asked to go with Pastor Tomas to pick up the adobe bricks we would need to fill the gaps in the walls of the barn's second story. Tom thought it was going to be very simple, and he didn't think twice about jumping in one of the vehicles that hadn't had any work done on it yet. Driving out of Rio Chico, he had an opportunity to see the mountains from a new vantage point and was overwhelmed by the beauty of this area. He said they turned off the highway onto a dirt road and finally came to a village that was in the middle of nowhere. All the homes were of adobe construction and behind one of them were thousands of handmade adobe bricks. They bought as many as would fit into the trailer and bed of the pickup truck and loaded them up. As Tom got back into the truck he considered the weight of their load and wondered if the truck could handle it.

At one point in their journey, they passed Kevin and Juan who were on their way to Madera for truck parts. Juan stopped the truck they were driving to talk to Pastor Tomas on one of the steep grades, but of course, Pastor Tomas couldn't stop. He gave his brother in the other truck a funny look and wave, and kept on going. When Davy and Sam looked at the truck later, Davy said there were no brakes left on the vehicle at all. Jorn then told Pastor Tomas he didn't want any of us riding in any of the trucks until Davy and Sam declared them safe.

Diane and I took a break together that afternoon and walked up the mountain behind the house. We could not get away without the children though. They wanted to come along and often ran ahead of us. I have to admit that, for me, it was a bit unnerving to have them up there with us. With the ledges and crevices, the steepness of the mountain, and small rocks and pebbles that would roll under foot with each step, I feared that one of them would fall and get hurt. I was the one who fell on her butt though when those pebbles made my sneakers perform like roller skates. But the children were totally at home up there. They had the sure-footedness of their ancestors—the ability to run and to climb with the agility of a mountain goat. They delighted in appearing above us and yelling "Hola" (Hello) from various vantage points. The view from this place is just awe-inspiring. It gave me an even greater appreciation of God's wonderful handy work.

Again we could see the cross over on the next mountain, and it was in this area that Shawn had had a very special encounter with God

Tom – "On the way back to camp with the bricks, I realized that on the mountains, Pastor Tomas had geared the truck way down into creeper gear. We were just crawling down the mountains and I could smell what was left of the one working brake burning away. The motor of the truck was roaring in its attempt to hold the truck back. The roads were very steep with even steeper drop offs along the side. Many areas had no guardrails separating traffic from those drop offs. Something else that added to the intensity of the trip were the numerous catholic monuments to those who'd lost their lives along these very roads. I realized what we were doing was quite dangerous. The latch was broken on the inside of the door, so Josh kept his hand on the outside door handle in the event we had to make a hasty exit from the vehicle. Josh had his eyes closed most of the way down though. He said he was sleeping, but I'm sure he was just too afraid to watch. One thing that brought me comfort though, was that Pastor Tomas was driving and I knew God wasn't going to do him in."

during one of his early morning devotional times. It was a powerful experience with the presence of God that he will not soon forget.

Shawn – "On Tuesday morning I walked up on the mountain behind the house to spend some time alone with the Lord. I climbed to a high section of the mountain where I could look across the valley and see the cross high atop the other mountain. There I sat down on a rock. I was looking at the cross, far off in the distance and I was praying for the group when God spoke to me. He was clearly sharing His heart with me when He said, "Shawn, a lot of people wear a cross as a symbol around their neck, in their ears or on their t-shirt, but for many of them, their relationship with Me is as distant as that cross is to you." I was reminded then, of Peter when the Lord invited him to step out of the boat. The Lord felt as real and as close to me at that moment as He must have been with Peter. It was as if He was sitting there next to me, sharing His disappointment with me as a friend would. I hadn't experienced the presence of God like that in a long time. It was very powerful."

Later that evening, during our teaching time, Jorn taught from Genesis 3:1-13, the story of the serpent's deception of Adam and Eve. Jorn said deception means believing a lie that sometimes causes you to do things you later regret. You believe something about yourself that is not true or you believe something about God that is not true. God has a perfect plan for our lives, there is no plan B. When we get off track, He'll get us back on track if we'll let Him. Deception convinces us that we are right or righteous, or justifies our actions. Second Corinthians 11:14 reminds us that Satan dresses up as a beautiful angel of light. His goal is to keep us from living up to our potential. John 8:44 says that Satan is the father of lies and cannot tell the truth. He waits for an opportunity to attack.

Jorn told us in order to overcome the lie; we must be in the Word of God. We need to have a deep, intimate relationship with God, opening up our hearts to Him and being transparent with Him. It was food for thought for us all.

I believe that prayer of surrender at the river was significant to what would happen later in the week. God will always be with us as we surrender our hearts and lives to Him. He is anxiously waiting to take all we have to offer and make something beautiful out of the mess we've made in going it alone without Him.

Chapter Twelve

PRAYER FOR PROTECTION

by LeAnn

Davy led devotions on this day. He talked to us about the struggle he had with his decision to come on the trip. He wanted to find an excuse not to come, but in the end, he knew God wanted him to be here. Some of the scriptures that influenced his decision were: Luke 10:2—"What a huge harvest! And how few the harvest hands"; 1 Peter 1:24—"The old life is a grass life, its beauty as short-lived as wildflowers; Grass dries up, flowers droop, God's word goes on and on forever"; John 4:32-34—"He told them, I have food to eat you know nothing about. The food that keeps Me going is that I do the will of the One who sent Me, finishing the work He started." Davy told us it's important to be occupied with work that will last for eternity, to live our lives with an eternal perspective. He also shared with us about a note of encouragement he received from a member of our church. Those words of encouragement had meant so much to him and had touched him very deeply. He realized if something that simple could mean so much to him, how much more is what we do for

Kevin serving up one of Brenda's awesome meals

Pastor Tomas and Brenda going to mean to them.

When we gathered together for lunch that day, Denny didn't join us. Instead he chose to go up on the mountain behind the house to fast and to pray during that time. He was praying for our protection and for the miracle

Denny – "On Wednesday I felt a burden to fast during lunch and to go up on the mountain to pray. I went out the backdoor of the guesthouse and up on the mountain behind the house. I used the backdoor because I felt an urgency to pray for our protection, asking God to be our rear guard as we moved forward in Him. I prayed specifically for each member of our team, asking God to protect us from any schemes of the enemy. I also felt God wanted to do something special in church on Sunday because of what had happened the Sunday before. So I asked God to reveal Himself in a miraculous way in that service."

he felt God wanted to do on Sunday. Little did he know that the miracle he was praying for would involve all of us!

We all looked forward to coming back together in the evenings for fellowship after spending the day working in separate areas. Dinnertime and those evenings spent together as a group were such fun. We would talk about the events of the day and enjoy each other's presence. Then we would fall, exhausted, into our beds, looking forward to what tomorrow held.

God is with us as He provides a hedge of protection around our lives. Denny was praying for that hedge during our lunch break that afternoon, and many others would join him in praying that protection over all of us later in the week.

Chapter Thirteen

STRETCHED TO THE LIMITS

by Pastor Jorn

We faced a lot of challenges during the week. Everyone had difficult situations that pushed them to their limits, and we all had to deal with our hearts at times. That's the way a mission trip is—things are going to happen—but we were able to do a lot of really great work while we were there. At the same time, we ministered to each other and to those around us. Everyone worked so hard. From the time we got up, until it was dark, everyone was out working. They were all busy serving Pastor Tomas and doing it all as unto the Lord.

Kevin Snyder was our truck parts manager. It was his job to go into Madera and pick up the parts the mechanics needed, or tools and supplies needed at the barn. Before we left home, Pastor Tomas gave me a list of some of the parts he thought they needed. So before crossing the border into Mexico, we stopped at an auto parts store and purchased some of those things. We bought batteries, gas filters, and brake linings, but we did not have nearly all that was needed. Sam and Davy had to get creative with some of the parts and used them on vehicles for which they were not intended. They would go over one of the trucks each morning and give Kevin a shopping list of parts. The guys at the barn usually found themselves in need of a few things as well. Juan would take Kevin to town and help him with translation, but even with Juan's help, Kevin's job was quite challenging. He went to Madera for three days in a row and could not get any parts, but he didn't let it discourage him. There was no huge auto parts store like most of us have access to in the United States. They sometimes had to go to several different shops before they found what was needed. Another frustration was finding the shops locked up during siesta. Kevin persevered though and was the perfect man for the job.

While Kevin was gone, Davy and Sam were tearing everything apart. When I (Jorn) walked down to where they were working that afternoon, every truck was in pieces. Parts were laying everywhere and Davy said, "Well, hey, we're done!" Of course that only lasted about thirty seconds until I put them to work on something else.

Juan assisting with generator problems

One thing that was a constant struggle throughout the week was the unreliable electrical current. The tools ran at a slow speed, and if too many tools were used at one time, the breaker would be tripped. In rural Mexico, it is not like here in the United States. If we call the power company to report a problem, we can expect a repair truck to come within a couple of hours of our call. There, one could wait many days for help to arrive. So when the power went down late one afternoon, the guys looked to Juan for help. Juan looks the part of a true cowboy, from his black cowboy hat, to his big shiny belt buckle, to the spurs on his boots; but we didn't realize he had the skills to go with it. He came out carrying a lasso and very skillfully threw it around the X-beams between the electrical poles. Then, using the secured rope, he climbed to the top of the pole and flipped the breaker.

The restored power only lasted a short time though. When the power went down again, I decided to have a go at it. Juan had taken his lasso with him when he left, so we carried the ladder over from the barn. I climbed up to flip the breaker, but it was of little use. Shortly thereafter, we were in the dark again and discovered that the wire from the main line to the breaker had completely burned off. Back at the house, Brenda had to resort to plan B in her efforts to prepare our dinner, but it didn't faze her. She's used to dealing with the setbacks that can come with living in rural Mexico.

By this time it was dark, so Juan came back with the hat Sam had brought that had a light on it. While I held the ladder, Juan went back up on the pole and dug his spur into the ground wire. As sparks rained down on me, he proceeded to reconnect the wire directly to the live power line with a pair of pliers, bypassing the breaker. As he worked, he told us about a friend of his who had nearly been electrocuted when he tried something similar. The others held flashlights and prayed for Juan's protection. As soon as it was connected, our extension cords shorted out and caught fire. A huge ball of fire traveled across the cords to the neighbor's house, nearly setting the house on fire. Thankfully, though, the house was made of mud and the only damage was to the electrical box on the outside wall of the house. We had to wonder what was going through the occupants' minds as they watched the antics of this crazy bunch of gringos.

In a twist of irony, while the men worked on the electricity, Shawn reported seeing a power company truck on the road near the compound. Apparently, they felt we had everything under control because the driver did not stop. The power was finally restored, and Brenda was able to cook our dinner, thanks to Juan's brave efforts.

In the evening, I taught from Psalm 37:7a, "Be still before the Lord and wait patiently for Him" (NIV). We are to sit in expectation of what God is going to do in our lives. We sometimes miss what He's doing because He moves gently. When we don't wait on Him, we are walking in the flesh and He cannot be glorified in it. We are not to do anything in our own strength, but are to be led by the Spirit. Then, we are truly sons of God. This was another of those lessons that we would be called to live out later in the week.

God is with us in giving us wisdom. Kevin needed wisdom for spending our funds wisely and for the challenges he faced to meet our need for parts and supplies. The mechanics needed wisdom to be able to get those trucks back in running order when they didn't always have the proper parts. The guys at the barn needed wisdom for laying adobe bricks and welding, things some of them had never done before. Many times during the week we had to seek God's wisdom for the tasks before us, and He was faithful to provide it.

Chapter Fourteen

EVENING WITH PASTOR

by LeAnn

This morning, it was my turn to lead devotions. I told our group that when I was in Florida a couple of weeks before our trip to Mexico, I had spent a lot of time walking on the beach. As I walked, the coarse sand and broken shells hurt my bare feet, and I was reminded of the process by which pearls are formed. A grain of sand gets inside the oyster's shell, and the sand irritates the oyster. To soothe the irritation, it emits secretions which form the beautiful pearl around that grain of sand. In James 1:2-4 it says,

> *Consider it a sheer gift when tests and challenges come at you from all sides. You know that under pressure, your faith life is forced into the open and shows its true colors. So don't try to get out of anything prematurely. Let it do its work so you become mature and well developed, not deficient in any way.*

It's the stresses and irritations outside our comfort zones that bring us to maturity and there are no short cuts in that process. I told the group that we were all in that place this week. We were being stretched in a myriad of ways. For most of us, we were being stretched in ways that we could never have imagined. Like the pearl inside the oyster, God is molding us and shaping us into His perfect design.

As we gathered for supper that night, it was raining outside. It had not rained there in three months, and there was a rainbow in the sky. It seemed as if God was showing us that He was pleased with our sacrifice of love.

That evening we were blessed to sit under Pastor Tomas' teaching, and it stirred our hearts and minds so very deeply. He talked to us using Psalm 68:6, which had also been Jorn's text for Sunday's sermon. The verse, "God sets the lonely in families" (NIV), describes what Pastor Tomas is trying to do here and in the canyon. His vision is also connected to the verse that speaks of a hen gathering her chicks under her wings. It's a picture of how God longs to draw all people to Himself, in love and protection.

He expressed appreciation for our attitude and the joy we brought with us. He related it to Psalm 100:2 which says, "Bring a gift of laughter, sing yourselves into his presence." We had been doing that all week and the joy in our hearts came from doing the will of the Father. He said that even if we had done no work at all, it would have been a blessing to have us there, just to share in our joy. He told us that God fought for each of us to be there and He won, but we all benefited from that victory. We were all so blessed by what God had done to bring us together in this place. It was a blessing far greater than anything we were able to accomplish by being there. It was all about God and what He was doing in and through us.

He told us that the barn is important to the storage of hay and protection of the animals. The restored vehicles are also vital to his ministry to the Indians in the canyon. He said he believes our church has an understanding of God's heart. And he encouraged us always to give our best to God because He deserves the very best we have to give.

He said that Rio Chico is where he prepares for battle, and he feels it's significant that God sent us at the beginning of his ministry year. Psalm 101:6 says, "But I have my eye on salt of the earth people—they're the ones I want working with me; Men and women on the straight and narrow—these are the ones I want at my side." I am so glad we

> **Larry** – "That evening with Pastor Tomas touched my heart deeply. He was so grateful and overwhelmed by all we had done. He also expressed appreciation for the love we had for each other. One thing that really spoke to me was when he said that too often people don't give their best when they give to missionaries. They give what's left over, worn out or no longer needed, as represented by the trucks outside. He said those trucks are what they've been given to work with. I could tell his heart was carrying a heavy burden because of that attitude in people. He encouraged us to give our best when giving to missions because when you give to a missionary, you are giving to God and He deserves the very best we have to give. He also told us he believes our church shares his burden for the lost and vision for reaching them. He was clearly pouring his heart out to us and it was amazing to be a part of it."

are those people for Pastor Tomas. I will never forget that evening with him. God's presence filled the room as he spoke, and we were all overwhelmed with emotion. I wept uncontrollably. The tears were coming from a place deep inside me, and they couldn't be stopped. It was all part of a wonderful thing happening in the room that evening though. It was not just the words spoken, but as Diane would later say, it was about our hearts being torn in two so they could be knit together and become one with Pastor Tomas' heart.

We were also feeling the love of God for the Tarahumara Indians. Swirling through our minds were images of the Tarahumara Indians of centuries ago, the natives of the land, being driven deeper into the canyons, into even more difficult living conditions than they already had, by those who would discover the wealth of mining in the mountains. Yes, our work with Pastor Tomas was important work; and his desire to do God's work, combined with our desire to do the same, made the mission trip worth all the effort and hard work.

We really had gotten an amazing amount of work done in those few days. The guys at camp just don't have the time or the funds for anything beyond their normal duties, and we were so grateful to have had the opportunity to help them. We knew Pastor Tomas was overwhelmed by everything we had been done. One thing I'll always remember about Pastor Tomas was when we were all seated at the long dining room table, he would walk behind everyone and stroke the back of each person on his way by. He is a man of few words, but that gesture seemed to be his way of thanking and blessing each one for what they were doing.

God's presence was very evident to all of us as Pastor Tomas shared his heart with us that evening. The rain of the Holy Spirit was refreshing our spirits as the rain that was falling outside was being soaked up by the thirsty earth. Both were blessings being poured out by God, and the rainbow that followed the rain was a precious reminder of God's presence with us.

Tom putting down the barn floor

Jorn welding beams for stairs

Ben & Shawn putting finishing touches on stairs

Gilberto & Chico mixing cement

Jorn fixing Christian & Gabby's wheelbarrow

Tom with one of the completed gates

Off loading the adobe bricks

Josh mixing mud

Ben showing how it's done

Sam inspecting a well-worn tire

Davy hard at work

Sam & Davy after a hard day's work

Diane hitting the high spots

Diane & Denny, fellow painters

Shawn, Christian, Francisco & Larry building the steps

Chapter Fifteen

WALKING ALONE

by LeAnn

Larry led devotions that morning using John 6:27—"Don't waste your energy striving for perishable food like that. Work for the food that sticks with you, food that nourishes your lasting life, food the Son of Man provides. He and what He does are guaranteed by God, the Father to last."

Larry said he worked for self until he gave his life to God. Then his attitude changed. When he does something for God now, he is rewarded with peace and joy.

The things we do for God last for eternity. He told us he had sacrificed a hunting trip to go to Mexico. His friends could not understand why he would do that. John 6:67-69

> *Then Jesus gave the Twelve their chance: Do you also want to leave? Peter replied, Master, to whom would we go? You have the words of real life, eternal life. We've already committed ourselves, confident that you are the Holy One of God.*

We were enjoying what we were doing because we were in God's will. It's what He wanted us to do. Our heart's desire is to see this ministry succeed, and we are proud to have had a small part in that success.

Work was winding down over at the barn, so Shawn and Larry decided to build a new set of steps in front of the guesthouse. That morning they gathered everything they would need and went to work. Chico and Christian were assisting them when they heard horrible cries from up on the mountainside across from the barn. It sounded like a child screaming and Christian yelled, "Nino!" which means "small child." He and Chico dashed toward the sound. When they reached the scene, they were relieved to find it was a goat and not a child that was the source of those cries. It proved to be a stark reminder that despite the beauty of the mountain ridges, it could be dangerous.

Shawn – "When I heard the screams from the mountain and heard Christian say, "Nino", I immediately thought there was a mountain lion attacking one of the Mexican children. So I followed after the others, running as fast as I could. Kevin was nearby and heard it too. He took off after me, but when we arrived at the scene of the cries, we found a goat being attacked by one of the neighbor's dogs. I looked at Kevin and said, "You mean we just ran 300 yards for a goat?" When Jorn came in at lunchtime, he came to me; his face filled with concern and asked what caused all the excitement earlier. He said he had never seen me run so fast and I had to explain that all that effort was for the rescue of a goat."

Juan and Kevin began making their trips to town a little earlier in the day to avoid being there during siesta and were eventually able to purchase all the required parts. Kevin also used his bargaining skills to get some pretty good deals in the process. Thanks to Kevin's hard work, Davy and Sam had what they needed and were finishing up their work that morning. The guys at Rio Chico use three trucks primarily. Those were the ones we were asked to repair. Davy and Sam practically rebuilt those trucks. Brakes, steering columns, ball joints, you name it—they fixed or replaced it. Not only had they fixed all three of those vehicles, but they managed to repair three other trucks as well. In addition to repairing the trucks, they reconnected the gas lines to original specifications and equipped each truck with a locking gas cap and its own battery. They had a ball doing it too. As the work on each truck was completed, we would hear them roar out of the yard and up the mountain, knowing Davy and Sam were taking another finished truck out for what they hoped would be a successful test drive. Those vehicles are probably working better now than when they were given to them, thanks to Davy and Sam's hard work. And the rest of us no longer had to worry about the brakes failing on their way back down the mountain!

It was the final day of work for Denny, Diane, and me too, so we got right to it. We were hoping to finish up by noon so we could have the afternoon off to hike up to the cross. We met our goal, finishing up the painting and cleaning the upstairs soon after lunch. We went outside to see how the work was progressing at the barn, with the vehicles, and on the steps. Afterwards we asked Pastor Jorn if it would be all right if we would go for a hike to the cross. Trips between the house and barn all week were just not satisfying my craving for walking. I could not wait to get out on the trail. Denny had been to the cross before using a shortcut. He and Diane started out in that direction, but I was ready to hike and, for me, a shortcut was just not going to do. I wanted to go the long way and told them I would meet them at the cross. So I walked off, leaving Denny and Diane staring after me. I had no idea that I was walking right into an incredible plan and miracle of God that would take me through the next two days.

I thought nothing of walking off alone because I have gone hiking alone before, and the guys had been hiking in the mountains all week without incident. As I walked along the path, I remember talking to the Lord about how grateful I was to be there. It was wonderful to finally have the opportunity to get out into the middle of His beautiful creation and not have to longingly gaze at it from afar. It was as if He was right there next to me, and we had set out on this adventure together.

Diane – "As I watched LeAnn walk away from us, she was silhouetted by dark trees; but there was light in front of her and she was walking toward it. I felt that she was walking into the light of Jesus."

I walked along a lovely creek that meandered along the base of the mountain before turning into the woods. The path to the cross was unmarked, and I missed it. Instead, I inadvertently followed a horse trail up over the mountain. After awhile, I realized I was probably not on the right path, but I was captured by the beauty around me. I simply couldn't make my feet turn and go back the way I had come. The anticipation of seeing what was beyond the next rise kept me moving forward. Each time I came across another breathtaking view, I'd tell the Father how beautiful it was, and He seemed to say, "Yes, I know, I made it."

I assumed that when I reached the top of the mountain, I would be able to see the cross and planned to just head in that direction. Once at the cross, I would be able to return to camp the other way. I did not have a watch with me and soon lost track of the time. When I realized I was not going to be able to see the cross from where I was and I was going to have to turn around to go back the way I had come, it was already too late.

I turned and hurried back down the trail, but I was only about half way back when darkness fell. I could no longer see the trail due to the dense forest in that area. I sat down for a minute and thought about my situation, considering what I needed to do. I know you are supposed to stay where you are

Last shot before starting back to camp

when you get lost, but I could hear what I thought was the river behind me. I was convinced that if I could get to the river, I would be able to follow it back to camp. I asked God to "be a light unto my path" and when I looked behind me, the moon was shining on a path I hoped would lead me to the river. So I stood up and began to follow the path.

It was difficult going in the dark with just the sound of the water to guide me. At one point, I found myself in a very dense area where there once may have been a spring. Much to my dismay, I found myself there again a little while later. I found another route out of that area, but it was quite steep. Back up on a narrow path, my footing gave way and I fell to my side. I grabbed onto some type of vegetation, but it didn't hold my weight and I slid down the embankment. I didn't know what was below me or how far I might fall, but in the time it took to breathe the name of Jesus, my downward slide was stopped. Although a bit dirtier, I was unhurt. Somehow, I finally reached the foot of the mountain and was relieved to find myself at the river, although I am not exactly sure how I got there. I started walking downstream, but before long, I came to a deep pool of water with rock walls on either side that I could not get through.

I crossed the river, which was barely more than ankle deep due to the lack of rain. I started up the ridge on the other side thinking I might be able to find a way around the deep pool. It was not long before I came to a place where the direction of the path was unclear. I knew it was too dangerous to be walking around on the ridge at night, so I stood up there for a while considering what to do next. It was already very cold, and I longed for warmer clothing. I knew I was not far from camp because I could hear the dogs barking in front of me, and traffic on the highway to my right.

Until that moment I had not considered the fact that I might not be able to make it back to camp on my own, and I realized I was in trouble. I began yelling for help and heard my cries repeated as they echoed through the canyon. I thought the others would hear my voice and come find me any minute. As the minutes wore on and I began to tire, I looked for somewhere to rest. I found a rock that I thought might serve well as a backrest. When I put my hand on it, I was surprised to find it soft and subtle. It felt like there was a thick blanket of sheepskin covering the rock. At the time I assumed it was moss that made it feel soft. Thinking back though, I do not remember seeing moss anywhere else during my wanderings on the mountain. Could it be that God had supernaturally provided a soft resting place for His lost sheep that night?

The night didn't get completely dark due to the brightness of the full moon. I was very grateful for its light. The night, however, was very cold and seemed endlessly long. As I sat there shivering, my thoughts were with the team. I imagined how concerned they must be. I knew they would be praying and looking for me, but I heard nothing. Not wanting to cause anyone to worry, I prayed no one else would find out about my ordeal until after I was found. I was determined to stay awake and tried to call out every five to ten minutes. I didn't know what effect the cold would have on my body so I also attempted to keep wiggling my fingers and toes. Of course I was praying and I tried to sing, but could not force the words past my chattering teeth. Instead, I began to meditate on the devotional and teaching times we had together during the week, which thankfully were very fresh in my mind. After awhile, frustrated by not hearing any response to my calls for help, I began screaming the name of Jesus. When it was obvious the others were not hearing my voice, I knew Jesus would and that brought me such peace.

I know God was with me when I walked away from camp that afternoon. I had no idea what lay up the path for me, but He did and He wasn't going to allow me to go alone. He's always with us and He always knows what's ahead for all of us. Not only that, but He's not limited by time either. He's eternal, so He's already been where we are going and has prepared the way in advance.

Chapter Sixteen

FRANTIC SEARCH

by Pastor Jorn

When Sam and Davy finished with the trucks that afternoon, they made their way up to the cross as well and caught Denny and Diane kissing while they waited for LeAnn. They had not had much opportunity to be alone all week and were making good use of their time while they waited! At 5:00, it was starting to get dark, so they all came back down to camp thinking that LeAnn had given up her pursuit of the cross and had returned to camp another way. When they got back, they came to me and told me LeAnn had not met them at the cross. At first, I (Jorn) was not concerned and did not consider that she might be lost. Instead, I thought she was somewhere around the buildings. After a search of the buildings and not finding her, I went to Brenda with the news. She said, "It's all right Jorn, we'll find her. She probably just got off the path. That's easy to do here." She and Pastor Tomas were very calm and confident LeAnn would be found quickly. They were convinced she was close by, but possibly could not get back to camp due to an injury.

As soon as the others heard that LeAnn was lost, everyone took off in search of her. My team, the Mexicans, everyone was searching. Some thought she just got off the path and others thought she might have gotten trapped in a ravine or crevice somewhere. As darkness fell, we started to believe she might have gotten hurt because we had been all over the mountain, screaming her name, and had gotten no response. There were guys at both ends of the mountain with flashlights, and they could see and hear each other. Some were a couple of miles away, and they could still be heard screaming and blowing the whistle. In the stillness of that night you could hear their voices for miles, but we heard nothing from LeAnn.

Shawn's whistle was not the only thing we had brought with us to Mexico that came in handy that night. Sam had brought the hat with a "head" lamp. Denny and Diane had brought ten "shake and light" flashlights. Tom had brought walkie-talkies, and Davy had brought a satellite phone. We believe

God prompted these persons to bring these items and the importance of each became very evident as the night wore on.

Later, around 8:30 or 9:00, we decided to call everyone in from the mountains. My guys were running all over the mountain. Emotions and adrenaline were running high, and I was concerned someone else might get lost. Pastor Tomas and I decided it would be best to pair my team members up with one of the Mexicans who were familiar with the area. Finally, we were able to yell loudly enough to get everyone back to camp, but still, no one had found LeAnn. After breaking them up into search parties, we sent them back out on the moun-

Shawn – "Late that afternoon, when we were finishing up our work, Jorn called us all together and asked if anyone knew where LeAnn was. No one knew, so he sent us out to look for her. Amazingly, God had put it on my heart to buy a combination whistle, magnifying glass and compass before I came on the trip. At the time I couldn't imagine why I would need it, but I bought it anyway thinking one of the kids might like to play with it. When we finished with the steps, I gave it to Christian, but when I heard LeAnn was lost; I went to him and told him I needed it back to aid in my search for LeAnn. I was all over the mountain blowing that whistle, but we couldn't find her anywhere. We came back to camp later to regroup, hoping someone else had found her, but no one had. We knew then that it was serious, very serious. It was very cold and it was difficult to stay warm, even as we were hiking through the mountains with our coats on. We all began to feel the urgency of the situation. When I thought of LeAnn being out there alone, I determined in my heart that I would look for her as I would for my wife if she were lost. That was the attitude I took with me and I believe we all had that attitude as we were searching."

tain, hopefully to search in a more organized manner this time.

The Mexicans were searching just as hard as we were, if not harder. Some were out until the wee hours of the morning and went back out again with only a couple of hours sleep. Gonzalo had gotten back from his trip into the canyon that afternoon and found us in the midst of our crisis. He immediately joined in the search. Juan and Ramon spent nearly all night out on horseback. The Mexicans and Indians were also excellent trackers. Josh and Ben were

Ben – "Josh and I were with Tomas Friday night, when we walked up around the mountain and ended up at the cross. Tomas had a big spotlight with him and he decided to go up on the little ledge that surrounds the cross so he could look down into the crevices along the cliff face. Tomas, wearing cowboy boots, inched his way around the cross, shining the spotlight into the crevices 150 feet below. Afraid Tomas was going to fall; Josh and I turned and walked the other way so we wouldn't have to watch should he loose his footing on his precarious perch. We knew that if he fell, he would probably not survive it. "

We covered a lot of area that night. Some of the guys left in the van with Brenda and Rosenda. They went to all the homes they knew of in the area, hoping to find someone who had seen or heard from LeAnn. They drove all over the mountains in the area. They navigated tiny overgrown dirt roads and would suddenly come across a little adobe shack with a whole family living inside. It was the middle of the night, but Rosenda

walking back along the creek with Pastor Tomas on Friday night when Pastor Tomas found what he said was a small footprint. Ben looked at the spot but saw only stones. Pastor Tomas then found another and started to follow the tracks up the creek bed. Josh and Ben just fanned out and followed behind, but neither saw anything resembling a footprint. He was probably following the tracks LeAnn had made earlier in the week when she had walked back there during one of her devotional times.

Tom – I was probably the closest one to the river when we were going up over the mountain that night. I heard a noise and hoping it was LeAnn, I started off toward it. When I got to where I thought the sound originated though, I found myself at the edge of a very high cliff with one of Pastor Tomas' goats. I looked down and could see flashlights carried by other team members who were searching along the river. There were several times when I heard a noise or the dogs that were with us would take off and we'd expect to find her in that direction. When we went to investigate though, our hopes were dashed time and time again. We were on an emotional roller coaster. It was a night filled with suspense and anxiety."

would make her way to the door, navigating a path through the inevitable dogs. After her knock, a candle would flicker inside the home, and someone would come to the door. No one had seen LeAnn, but they all offered to help with the search the next day. Everyone in the area was committed to trying to find her.

God had been with us even as we were packing and deciding what to bring along to Mexico. Several team members had brought items that would be very valuable to us during the search. God is with us when He prompts us to prepare for what lies ahead even when we don't know what that is. When what He's telling us doesn't seem to make sense, we need to trust Him and obey His word anyway.

Chapter Seventeen

WHERE, OH WHERE?

by Pastor Jorn

We had spent hours searching and everyone had done all they knew to do to find LeAnn. They were blowing the truck horns. They screamed until they had no voices left. They hiked up and down the mountains until their muscles were screaming as loudly as their voices, but they could not find her anywhere.

Tomas and Brenda were baffled. Tomas came to me sometime during the night and said, "Jorn, I have no idea where she is." He knew the path she had taken and had looked in all the logical places along the path and had not found her. They also could not understand why the two Tarahumara Indians, who were excellent trackers, had found no sign of her. These men are so gifted in tracking they can tell when a pebble has been turned over, yet they had not found any evidence of her being up on that mountain. When he told me these things, I (Jorn) began to think about all the possible scenarios. *Could she have been kidnapped? Had she decided to walk along the road and was picked up by someone? Had someone found her injured and taken her somewhere for treatment?* There were a number of possibilities going through our minds. Tomas and Brenda still were not too concerned though. They were convinced we would find her when we continued our search in the morning.

I had that hope as well and decided it was time to call my team back to camp for some much needed rest. They did not want to come in. They wanted to stay out and continue their search. They wanted to be doing something, anything, to help LeAnn. I explained that the Indians and Mexicans were familiar with the area and for that reason, were much better suited to search the darkness than we were. I told them I did not want to risk anyone else getting hurt or lost, and insisted they all go to bed.

I knew they were worried and afraid, so before they went to their rooms I spoke to them. I told them there was plenty of opportunity to be afraid. We could easily crumple under the weight of the circumstances, curl up in a ball and cry, or lose hope because of what had happened. We could also allow the devil to fill our minds with all kinds of crazy scenarios of what might have happened to LeAnn. Doing so would only cause us to be fearful. Ultimately, we either allow those feelings to dictate our lives or we learn to control them through the power of Christ and the revelation of His Word working in our hearts. I assured them that if they could trust God and not their feelings, they would be able to stay sensible and not get crazy. I shared with them the truth that God was in control, and He would take care of LeAnn.

Later I went to talk to Denny and Diane. I did not want them to think LeAnn's disappearance was their fault in any way. I asked them not to think they had abandoned LeAnn or had done something wrong. I assured them this was not their fault. I reminded them that they were not looking after a 15-year-old girl. LeAnn knew what she was doing and had made her own decision to go off by herself.

We all had a lot to think about when we went off to bed. Some said they did not feel right about finding warmth in a comfortable bed, knowing LeAnn was out there somewhere without either warmth or comfort.

When I finally went to bed, I was, of course, praying for and thinking about LeAnn. The others were on my mind as well. I wondered what we would have done if one of the others had been lost. I thought about how they might have responded if they were the ones in LeAnn's shoes that night. My wife and I had known LeAnn since she joined our small group when she started coming to our church. We have been a part of her life since then. Because of the time we had spent with LeAnn, I knew beyond a shadow of a doubt that she had a quality relationship with Jesus. I knew Jesus was at the center of her life and that she was going to lean on Him in the midst of whatever struggle she was going through. I also knew the heavenly Father was going to be there with her no matter what. Thinking about LeAnn and her relationship with the Lord gave me comfort and peace, even though I didn't know what we would be going through over the next couple of days.

> **Davy** — "When I went to bed that night, I was thinking about how well our week had gone. Everyone was there to serve God and everything we set out to do was being accomplished. But if that was the case, I wondered how could this have happened? Questions like, 'How could LeAnn be missing?' and 'Why would God allow this to happen?' raced through my mind. I'm sure others had the same questions, but we all kept them to ourselves."

As was thinking about what had happened to LeAnn and the fact that she had this wonderful relationship with Jesus, it was natural for me to think about the parable of the lost sheep in Luke 15. It says,

65

Suppose one of you had a hundred sheep and lost one. Wouldn't you leave the ninety-nine in the wilderness and go after the lost one until you found it? When found, you can be sure you would put it across your shoulders, rejoicing and when you got home, call in your friends and neighbors saying, celebrate with me! I've found my lost sheep.

When I think about this passage of scripture, it is in the context of the lost because it talks about sinners who are away from God. But God chases the sheep that are saints too. He comes after us and woos our hearts every time we are away from Him. Every time we try to get away from God, He's there, chasing after us. He never leaves us alone. He searches for us as a good shepherd would. He leaves everyone of us in the comforts of our relationship with Him to go find the one who is lost.

I knew the good shepherd was with LeAnn, and I was never really afraid. I knew if I allowed my feelings get the best of me, the others would sense it and respond in the same way, in fear and hopelessness. I did not want them to think I was giving up or losing hope. There were times, though, when I was pretty solemn, lost in my own thoughts. My biggest struggle, by far, was the thought of having to break the news to the people back home, our church family and especially, LeAnn's family. How would I explain to her parents that she was missing and had possibly lost her life? I knew they would be understandably upset. I wrestled with the thought of having to explain to them what had happened. How could I possibly make those back home comprehend the situation when I was here, in the midst of it all and didn't understand it myself? When those of us in Rio Chico tried to examine the circumstances logically, we realized there was no way this should have happened. She could not have gotten far. We should have been able to find her. There was just no logical explanation for her being lost. But LeAnn's parents and others would want to know how this happened and I had no answers for them. I also knew there was the possibility that some might be angry. We could be blamed for what had happened, or thought to be responsible in some way. I was in charge, and it was my responsibility to watch over the people I had brought with me. I felt the weight of that responsibility. It was impossible not to feel it. It was a very difficult time, but I was not really afraid. God gave me the grace I needed to deal with the crisis in Rio Chico and with those who were hurting back home.

Where was God that night as we searched in vain to find LeAnn? We may not have seen Him move in our situation to find her that night, but we knew He had not forsaken us. He hadn't left us. He was right there alongside us and with LeAnn too.

Chapter Eighteen

LONG COLD NIGHT

by LeAnn

As I sat there, shaking from the cold, I thought about what Jorn had told us on Sunday morning just after arriving in Juarez. He told us that God is a good God and wants to give us good gifts. Jorn had encouraged us to search out the desires of our hearts, ask God for those things, and remind God of what we had done for Him this week and the sacrifices we had made to be there. As I contemplated the desires of my heart, I decided the thing I wanted most at that moment was my life. I also thought about Kevin's devotional when he talked to us about the scripture that says, "No greater love hath any man than he would lay down his life for his friends." He said we had laid down our lives by leaving our families and our lives back home, but I wondered, *is God going to ask me to literally lay down my life on this trip?* As I considered the possibility that I might die, I thought, *what better time to go than when we had been serving God whole heartedly as we had this week.*

My signature Psalm is Psalm 139, and I thought about those words a lot that night. It says,

> Helen Philips (a member of Grace Covenant/Lewistown) – "I had just gotten home from a late night at work when God spoke to me. He simply said, 'Pray for LeAnn'. We have a rather large church and I didn't know LeAnn Hartzler. Nor did I know what was happening in Mexico. I knew another woman by that name though and began praying for her. The next morning when I heard what was happening, I realized God had asked me to intercede for LeAnn even before anyone back in the states knew of her plight."

67

Where can I go from your Spirit, where can I flee from Your presence? If I go up to the heavens, You are there; if I make my bed in the depths, You are there. If I rise on the wings of the dawn, if I settle on the far side of the sea, even there Your hand will guide me, Your right hand will hold me fast (NIV).

I knew beyond any doubt God was with me in that secret place and His hand was on me. The passage also says,

If I say, surely the darkness will hide me and the light become night around me, even the darkness will not be dark to You; the night will shine like the day, for darkness is as light to You (NIV).

The bright full moon represented God's light in that dark place, and I was convinced God knew exactly where I was, even when the others did not. Many times during the night, I asked God to reveal my whereabouts to Pastor Jorn and Pastor Tomas.

The last few verses of that Psalm were also part of my prayers that night. "Search me, O God, and know my heart; test me and know my anxious thoughts. See if there is any offensive way in me, and lead me in the way everlasting" (NIV). I asked God to forgive me for anything I had done that had displeased Him, and I knew He would be faithful to do that. Because of my faith in, and acceptance of, Jesus' sacrifice for my sin, I also knew that if I did not survive the night, I would wake up in His presence. Whether I was to live or die, as I sat there I was at peace with either outcome. But when I thought about my family, my nephews that I love so much, my friends, my teammates, Pastor Jorn, Pastor Tomas, and the others who would feel so responsible if I did not survive, I asked God to spare my life.

The night was very cold. My body shook uncontrollably most of the time. I assumed this was my body's attempt to stay warm, so I did not fight it. I broke some branches off a nearby tree to cover myself, but because they were so sparse, the covering did not offer much help in conserving my body heat. I pulled my hands up into the sleeves of my sweatshirt and pulled the neck of the shirt up over my face, but I was still very cold. I prayed that God would somehow provide me with warmth: an animal to lie next to me, an angel, or His warm and loving arms, it did not matter. I desperately wanted some relief from the cold. I did not see any animals, but I knew He had his arms around me. I also believe He also sent an angel to comfort me that night. A woman from the Mount Union church, whom I had never met, told me later that when their church had met to pray for me, she had a vision of a woman, with hair exactly like mine, sitting among some rocks. Standing behind the woman was an angel, with his wings stretched out over her.

I had no idea how cold it was, but I was told later that it was somewhere in the twenties. It occurred to me that many of the Tarahumara Indians live in much the same conditions all winter long and here I was lamenting over having to spend one night in the cold. Their homes are barely more than what I had for shelter on this cold night. My experience was allowing me to identify with their suffering. I know in my heart that only God could have sustained me through those cold, long hours as I watched the moon creep ever so slowly across the night sky.

The next morning when the sun came up and I realized I had survived the night, I had an overwhelming assurance that I would be rescued. There was no doubt at all in my mind about that. One evening Jorn had taught on fear. He told us that faith and fear are opposites, which cannot coexist. That is exactly what I experienced. I had a supernatural faith that God would rescue me and there was absolutely no room for fear in my heart.

God was with me throughout that long cold night, and He was with me in the hope and faith He put in my heart for my rescue.

Chapter Nineteen

GO NOW!

by Pastor Jorn

Very early Saturday morning, while it was still dark, Davy and I (Jorn) went outside to use the satellite phone. I knew I couldn't put off that dreaded call to Pastor Ron back in Lewistown any longer. It was very cold outside. Within minutes I was shaking from the cold. My heart ached with the thought of LeAnn spending the whole night out in these conditions. I looked with dismay at the ice that had formed on the puddles during the night. I knew that unless God took care of LeAnn, she could have frozen to death. That was one of the most difficult phone calls I have ever had to make. When Ron picked up the phone, I said, "Ron, you've got to listen to me," and I proceeded to tell him what had happened. After his initial shock we both realized we had things we needed to do, so our conversation was brief. I had my responsibilities in Rio Chico concerning our efforts to find LeAnn, and Ron had matters to take care of back home.

As soon as there was enough daylight, we all resumed our search. I went out with Gonzalo and a couple of the other guys from the team. We looked everywhere. We went down to search along the river, but we found no sign of her. The guys wanted to keep going further upriver, but we turned around when Gonzalo said that area had been searched the night before.

That morning during the search, Ben had a close encounter with one of the cactuses that are called "Cowboy Killers." A sharp spine had pierced the skin of his leg through his jeans and the cut continued to bleed due to his physical exertion. When the flow of blood reached his boot, he asked Tom if he had a Band-Aid. Having none, Tom offered his handkerchief to tie around his leg. Thankfully his injury was just a flesh wound and was the only injury sustained by any of those searching for LeAnn.

The others were all out scouring other areas. Sam, Denny, and Diane were searching a ravine. Thinking that LeAnn, by this time, might be dehydrated or have some injury, they walked so they could see each other most of the time.

They kept checking the ground between them to make sure she was not laying there, hurt or unconscious. Suddenly, Diane found herself alone and unable to hear her husband or Sam. While she knew they could not be too far away, it was a frightening moment for her. Not wanting to join the ranks of the lost, she calmed herself and made the decision to walk up the side of the ravine where she found the men.

Not only were we all out looking, but others from the surrounding area poured in to camp to offer their assistance. The men came to help with the search; and the ladies came, bearing food to sustain those who were searching. I am sure these people were not wealthy. Some may have had barely enough food to feed their own families, yet they came, ready to share what they had to meet the needs of others. Pastor Tomas and Brenda had never experienced such an outpouring of love and support from the people of that area and were overwhelmed by it. They said it was as if these people had adopted LeAnn as their sister. Their efforts to find her matched our own, and they had never met her.

When it became apparent we were not going to find her again that morning, Pastor Tomas decided it was time to call the authorities. He thought with more manpower, we would be able to find her. Around lunchtime, the police came to help. An investigator came with them, and I had to answer a lot of questions about LeAnn's disappearance with the help of Brenda who interpreted for me. After looking around the camp for a while, he came back to us with still more questions. He wanted to know about my team, who we were and why we were there. Brenda coached me on what I should and should not say. She was concerned about our not having gotten visas on our way into Chihuahua because the Mexican government has a special visa for missionaries.

Ben – "The two deputies that came with the investigator reeked of alcohol. They had obviously been outfitted at an army surplus store. None of the pieces of their so called 'uniforms' matched. Nor did they match the 'Special Forces' description on their hats. They were not what we had pictured as our hoped for help and our spirits sank. They talked to Brenda for a few minutes and told her they would go get additional help. They then left, never to return. The first responders were quite a disappointment to us."

On my last trip with the teens in the summer, the authorities did not ask to see visas when we crossed the border, and I had asked Brenda if they were important or if they had ever had an issue with them. She told me they had always gotten them for their visiting groups, but had never been asked to show them. So I decided we could find a better use for the money we would save by forgoing the purchase of visas. Just like last time, we were not asked to show visas when we crossed the border, and so again, we had not gotten them.

I was not thinking about the visas, though, as I was standing before the investigator that morning. I was concerned for my team. After he asked about my team and why we were there, he asked to see LeAnn's passport, but he said nothing about not seeing a visa stamped on its pages. We all breathed a sigh of relief when he prepared to leave. He said he would be back later with more questions though. There was no time to consider what that meant or to worry because there was still much to do, and our focus was quickly returned to the search. The camp was a flurry of activity that morning.

> **Larry** – "We were all out searching on Saturday when we heard Jorn calling us. He said, 'We've got to get out of here and we've got to go now'. We didn't really understand what was going on, but because of the presence of all the authorities, Pastor Tomas told Jorn that he and the group should leave. I've never seen Jorn with such intensity on his face as he urged us to get our stuff together and get in the van. It was difficult to leave. It was the hardest part of the whole trip. I would have stayed there until LeAnn was found. Even if it took another week, it wouldn't have mattered. I wanted to stay there, and when he said we had to leave, man, it was tough."

A little later, Pastor Tomas came to me and said he felt it would be best to take the team back to Juarez because of our lack of visas to be in Chihuahua province. He explained that any repercussions for not having visas would fall on them and not on us, so I knew the authorities could not hold us for not having the visas. I was most concerned that they might want to hold my team on suspicion of foul play in LeAnn's disappearance. I did not want them subjected to questioning by the investigator and the anxiety it might cause, so I agreed it would be best to leave. The team was out searching, but finally, we were able to call them back to camp. I explained the situation to them and told them to collect their things as calmly and as quickly as possible. The next hour was pretty hectic as we got everyone and all our gear into the vehicles without raising the suspicions of the *policia*. The team didn't give me a hard time about leaving, although I knew they did not want to go. I explained what needed to be done, and they did what was required of them. I assured them others would continue to look for LeAnn. I reminded them that they did not know the area like the Mexicans do. The terrain is foreign to us, not at all like what we are used to in the mountains of Pennsylvania. I told them it would be best for us to just get out of the Mexicans' way and let them do their job without having to worry about someone else getting lost.

Before we left, Pastor Tomas came to me. He told me he had looked everywhere he thought LeAnn could possibly be and had found no sign of her. He said he didn't even know where else to look, but he assured us they would go back over all the areas that had already been searched. He suggested they could have missed something in the darkness the night before. He promised they would keep looking and would not give up until they found her. But, he added, "I have no idea where she is."

> **Brenda** – "It was a long, quiet trip back to Juarez. Some were crying and most were lost in their own thoughts. As I was driving, I thought, 'How sad it is to see this group that had come to Mexico with so much laughter and joy, leave with sadness and tears'. Pastor Tomas and I had come to love this group of people God had sent to help us. They had brought all of us so much love and joy. We didn't want to see their missions trip experience end like this."

Chapter Twenty

HEARTACHE AT HOME

by Pastor Ron

When Jorn called around 7:00 that morning to tell me what had happened, I (Ron) thought he was kidding. I thought he was playing a joke on me. I said, "Jorn, come on now." and he said, "No Ron, I'm serious." When he said that, I knew by the tone of his voice he was serious. My first thought was, *Oh my God! What now?* My second thought was that I had to get in touch with LeAnn's parents. I tried to calm myself and think rationally about my responsibilities as pastor in this crisis. I knew that Jorn had his responsibilities in Mexico as team leader, but what was it that I needed to do? I immediately started praying, asking God what I should do and asking for guidance as I stepped into those responsibilities. I realized my first responsibility was to try to reach her parents. I looked in the phone book for a number; however, I did not get an answer at their home. I knew her parents usually spend part of the winter in Florida, and it occurred to me they might be there. I also knew LeAnn had a family connection with the Werner family, so I called Sharon Werner to enlist her help in reaching LeAnn's parents. She told me they were in Florida and were staying right across the street from her mother-in-law. She said she would call her mother-in-law to get Lee and Fern's number and would call me back as soon as she could.

While I waited for Sharon to get back to me, I went in to the church where intercessors were gathered for our usual Saturday morning prayer. I explained the situation to our Pastor of Prayer, Roberta Aurand, and the others who were gathered. I asked them to pray for LeAnn, Jorn, and the rest of the team in Mexico. I also called Pastor Michael who was at the ministers' conference in Texas. He told me he would share our situation with the ministers there and ask that they pray as well. I found it amazing that God had placed Pastor Michael at that conference in Texas, just across the border from Mexico where our crisis was playing out. The ministers at the conference were providing prayer support right there, in the state that bordered Mexico, and our Pastor Michael was there to enlist that support.

Pastor Michael – "I was at a ministers' conference involving forty to fifty pastors and elders from the Texas district of Liberty Fellowship churches. I was at one of the host pastor's homes and we were just leaving for the morning session, when I got the call from Ron. The news came as quite a shock. I know and respect LeAnn's father and I immediately thought of myself in his shoes. I knew I didn't want our church to have any part in the loss of his little girl. As soon as the session began, I was able to enlist the prayers of those at the conference and we periodically took time out to pray for LeAnn throughout the rest of the conference. I felt it was ironic that I was in Texas, just across the border from Mexico where our crisis was happening. There were people at the conference who were missionaries in Mexico and I also called a missionary friend who lives in El Paso. He had worked in Mexico as a missionary and he cautioned me that this was a dangerous situation; that the wilderness areas could be strongholds for drug runners and all kinds of bad "hombres". I talked to people all over the country over those two days, asking them to pray and for any bit of information that might help us deal with our situation. I also called my daughter back home and asked her to send my passport overnight so I could go into Mexico to support Jorn."

Sharon called me later with the number for LeAnn's parents and told me she had also called one of our church members, Nicole Cavanaugh, who was spending a few months at the International House of Prayer in Saint Louis, Missouri. Intercessory prayer and worship happens there twenty-four hours a day, seven days a week. Nicole said she would ask her friends to include LeAnn in the constant prayer happening there.

I knew then that it was time to make the call to her parents. It was one of the most difficult calls I've ever had to make. When her father answered the phone, I told him who I was and that I had some news for him. He knew right away that something terrible had happened, and he repeated the words, "Oh, no." several times. I asked him to sit down and told him I had some things to tell him. Again, his only words were "Oh no." He knew I was serious and was trying to prepare him for what I was going to say. I shared with him all I knew about the situation and assured him we were praying and doing all we could possibly do to see LeAnn returned safely. It was not a long conversation, but I tried to encourage him with words of faith before we hung up.

Lee – "When Pastor Ron called that morning, I knew something terrible must have happened. My wife and I were shocked when he related the news of our daughter's disappearance. My wife immediately wanted to go home. I told her there was nothing we could do at home that we couldn't also do in Florida, but she insisted, saying she would call the airline if I did not. We were able to get a flight out later that afternoon, but in the meantime we were making phone calls. We first called our church's prayer chain and from there, the news spread quickly. We also called our son and the Marketing Department Manager for the insurance company where LeAnn works. He called LeAnn's supervisor and the company president. Due to their privacy policy, they decided they would not inform the other employees of LeAnn disappearance until they came in to work on Monday morning. That did not stop the others from finding out though. One of LeAnn's co-workers has a connection with one of my cousins who informed her. She called others who work closely with LeAnn, who in turn called still others, until quite a number of them knew what was happening. They were quite concerned for LeAnn's safety and were all praying and enlisting the prayers of their church families and friends as well.

Our flight out of Charlotte was overbooked and the airline was asking passengers to give up their seats, but there was no way we weren't getting on that plane. My brother and his wife picked us up in Harrisburg and it was snowing heavily as we drove home. We arrived home around 11:30 that night and went straight to bed, but didn't sleep much. Our thoughts were with our daughter, wherever she was."

I was considering trying get in touch with a government official in Washington when Lee called me back about thirty minutes later. He told me he had talked to his wife and that they had decided to return to Pennsylvania. They were leaving for the airport, so he gave me their cell phone number so I could stay in contact with them.

My brother Danny called me right after I got off the phone with Lee. His son, Josh, who was part of the missions team in Mexico, had called him with the news. Danny asked me what I was going to do, and I told him of my plans to try to reach someone in Washington. Danny suggested I call the US Embassy in Mexico instead. I realized his suggestion was a good one, and I went to the

Internet to see if I could find a phone number for the embassy. I found several numbers in Mexico City and called the first one I came to. This number connected me to an answering service, which provided me with another number to call. I finally reached a woman named Cynthia at the US Consulate. Carefully, I explained to her what was happening.

I told her about Pastor Tomas' ministry to the Tarahumara Indians and about his base camp in Rio Chico. I told her I did not know exactly where LeAnn was lost, but that it was somewhere near the camp at Rio Chico. She seemed to be familiar with the area because she knew it was in the Province of Chihuahua. She said she would talk to the authorities there to find out what was happening on the ground. She assured me she would go to work on it, and we exchanged contact information.

We were having our Hand of Grace food distribution at church that day. My wife, Cyndi, helps with administration duties at the distribution. Before she had to leave, we decided to talk to our children about what was happening in Mexico. We talked to our oldest son, Ryan, separately from the two younger children. He knows LeAnn because they are both a part of the worship team, so we told him about her disappearance first. I told him it was a very serious situation and asked him to pray for her rescue. I told him it was a matter of life or death, and he understood that.

Cyndi – "LeAnn normally helps with the administration of the food distribution as well, so her presence was missed that day. All the workers were praying for her as they worked throughout the day. The phone was ringing almost constantly with people calling to ask if what they had heard was true and if we had any further news. It was a somber day and no one had much to say. When something was said about the situation though, it was not negative. If someone asked, 'What if she was abducted?', someone would respond by suggesting that then, at least, she would be warm. Everyone remained positive and there was a sense that everything would be okay."

We asked the two younger children if they knew LeAnn, but they weren't sure at first. When we explained she has blonde hair and is on the worship team, they realized who she was. I simply explained to them that LeAnn was lost, and we were doing all we could to find her. We felt that was all they needed to know for the time being. They know their daddy well enough to know when something is seriously wrong, so both Cyndi and I felt we had to tell them something. They understood I was dealing with something serious that day, and they were good about playing on their own while I went about my day. If I wasn't on the phone with someone, I was praying. I'm not even sure I ate at all that day.

There were numerous conversations with Cynthia at the consulate. After the first couple of phone calls with her, I called LeAnn's parents to relay the information. Later though, I asked that she call them personally to let them know what she was doing, and I gave her their contact information. After that she began calling both of us. She remained very helpful throughout the whole ordeal. During one of our phone conversations, I asked her if she was a "believer." I was encouraged when she told me that she was. It was comforting to know that this woman, with whom I had to work so closely during this crisis, shared my belief in God.

In one of the later calls I had from her she told me, "It seems like the authorities are doing everything they can possibly do." She said they had mobilized a number of police officers and their equivalent of the National Guard in that area. She said that was an exceptional thing because those groups do not normally work together in Mexico. She told me they would also be providing a helicopter to aid in the search. Unfortunately, the helicopter had a mechanical problem, and they were never able to get it off the ground, but her words gave us hope in the midst of our trouble. In one of my conversations with Jorn, I asked how much help they had. He told me there were about fifty police officers, either searching the mountains around Rio Chico or questioning people and searching the hospitals in the surrounding towns.

My wife teases me about it, but when our phone is used a lot, sometimes it does not dial properly. Cyndi has never had the problem, so she's convinced the problem is with me and not the phone. But at one point on Saturday, I was trying to call Cynthia at the consulate, and I got a wrong number. A young woman answered and I asked if she was Cynthia from the consulate in Mexico. She said no, and that I must have the wrong number. I told her who I was and why I was trying to call the Mexican consulate. She told me that her parents were missionaries and that she had grown up on the mission field. She said she was now involved in her local church in Neffsville, Pennsylvania and I exclaimed, "My last name is Neff!" I asked her to please pray for LeAnn, and she assured me she would. I knew Pastor Michael and those at the ministers' conference were praying, and I knew the churches in LeAnn's hometown were praying. I saw this as an opportunity to have another area where churches were praying for LeAnn, and I asked her to request the prayers of her church family. It was kind of an odd conversation, but it encouraged me. I felt our phone call was a divine connection, orchestrated by God to encourage me and to enlist the prayers of still more Christians around the country.

My phone at home was ringing constantly. Everyone was concerned and wanted to know what was happening. More than once, I had my home phone to one ear and my cell phone to the other. There were lots of phone calls that day: calls to Cynthia, calls to LeAnn's parents, and calls from church members. At the end of the day, my ears literally hurt from being on the phone all day. Saturday was a day full of phone calls and prayer. That's basically what I did all day—pray and talk on the telephone, while my children entertained themselves.

Later that afternoon, after Hand of Grace, several ladies met at the church to pray for LeAnn and to organize a 24-hour prayer vigil. Within a couple of hours they had every time slot for the next twenty-four hours filled with someone willing to devote that time to prayer for LeAnn and for the rest of the missions team in Mexico. In this way our congregation would be joining their hearts with the round the clock prayer effort that was happening in Missouri.

As I pondered the situation, I always had a sense that LeAnn was just lost somewhere. Some people called and asked if she could have been kidnapped. I knew that was a possibility. It is hard not to, at least, consider suggestions like that. I thought she could have run into someone who may have abducted her, and yet, the feeling I had was that she was just lost. I thought she was possibly in a cave or cleft of a rock where she was hidden from view, but I didn't think anything sinister had happened to her.

I had already started on a sermon for Sunday morning, but I put that aside for another time. Saturday evening, I started planning for our morning worship service. I utilized the Internet again to find some maps that would help the congregation visualize the type of terrain where LeAnn was lost. I knew I would need to begin the service by explaining to the congregation that LeAnn was missing, but I also had to decide how we would handle the rest of the service. I knew immediately that I would not preach, but we would have a harp and bowl type of service instead, with much prayer and praise. (For those of you who are not familiar with harp and bowl services, they are services filled with worship, praise, and intercessory prayer. The service is without format and free flowing throughout to allow the move of the Holy Spirit.) I discussed my idea with Wes Clemmer, our overseer and our worship team pastor. I asked him to help lead the praise along with Kirk Pry, our worship leader. I asked

Roberta, our Pastor of Prayer, and Eva Boob, our Director of Women's ministry, and wife of Sam Boob, who was part of the missions team in Mexico, to lead the prayer. I knew from the beginning that our entire focus would be prayer for LeAnn and the rest of the team in Mexico.

At the end of the day, I was emotionally exhausted. I just kept asking myself, *why hasn't she been found yet?* I was anxious and was still praying when I went to bed, but somehow I was able to get about five hours sleep that night. I got up around 6:00 the next morning with our morning worship service in mind.

God was with me that day, giving me guidance and direction as I coordinated communications with those in Mexico and as I was planning for the next day's worship service. He even encouraged me with that connection to the woman in Neffsville, which reminded me of His presence with us in the midst of our storm.

Chapter Twenty-One

STAY OR GO

by LeAnn

During the night, God had told me to go back to the river and by this time, I needed water. As soon as there was enough daylight to see the path, I retraced my steps to the river. We had been told not to even brush our teeth with the water that comes from the river, but I knew I had to take my chances to avoid dehydration. I asked God to protect me from anything nasty that might be lurking in the water and satisfied my thirst. It was very cold, crystal clear, and tasted quite good. I was very thirsty, but I do not remember ever feeling hunger, even though I had not eaten since lunchtime on Friday.

Throughout the night I had been praying that God would show Pastors Jorn and Tomas where I was. I fully expected to be found as soon as the sun came up that morning, but instead, I spent most of Saturday there by the river, just waiting for someone to find me. I either stood or sat in the sunshine and hoped someone, anyone, would hear my cries for help. All the while I was asking God what I should do, but the only response I heard was "Peace, be still." I was desperately clinging to the assurance I had for being rescued and wasn't allowing my emotions to lead my thoughts in any other direction.

The canyon was narrow in this area; twenty steps would probably take you from one side to the other. There were empty soda bottles and a circle of rocks that looked like they were used as a fire pit. Those signs made me believe people visited there quite often, and I so wished someone would come by that morning. It was a beautiful spot with the sun glistening off the canyon walls and making the water sparkle as it tumbled over the river rocks. It was just the sort of place I would very much enjoy visiting under other circumstances. Despite the beauty around me, I decided not to take any photos while I was lost because I did not think I would want any reminders of that time. Little did I realize that I would think about my ordeal nearly every day for months, even without the aid of photographs.

I spent all morning pacing between the mountains and the pool of water, wondering to do. I was not even sure where I had come down off the mountain the night before, so I could not retrace my steps. After awhile, I decided to try to go through the pool by stepping on rocks below the surface of the water along the edge of the cliff. I was not more than a few steps into it when I slipped and fell in the water. I wonder sometimes if God gave me a gentle push because it was not yet time for my rescue. I thought about swimming the rest of the way, but the water was so cold it took my breath away. I discarded that idea and chose the quickest route out, back to where I had started. Now soaking wet, I knew it was imperative that I get dry as quickly as possible, so I took off my jeans and sweatshirt and wrung them out. I also took off my socks and sneakers and laid them out on a rock to dry. I remember thinking my mother would not approve of my going barefooted in February! It warmed up quite nicely during the day and my clothes dried out pretty well as I stood in the sun, but my sneakers remained damp.

I also started making preparations for spending another night out there. I gathered some dried grass that had become lodged on a tree when the river was running much higher. I put it on the ground next to a rock I had chosen as my resting place, hoping the rock might retain some of the heat generated by the sun shining on it during the day. I also found a feedbag entangled on a tree. I decided it might be useful as a covering and I laid it next to the rock as well. Even though I was preparing for it, I desperately did not want to spend another night out in the wilderness. Later, when Jorn told me Juan had been searching for me along the river, we decided to ask him if he had seen my preparations, but he said he had not.

Another thing I did throughout my ordeal was to set deadlines. I thought about our original plans and was deciding when I would need to be found so that we could still follow through with those plans. We were going to leave sometime that morning so we could get back to Juarez in time to do some shopping in the evening. I thought it was probably already too late for the shopping; but I thought if I were found by noon we could still make it back to Juarez tonight, and Jorn could still preach in four churches as planned on Sunday.

When afternoon came and I no longer had direct sunlight in the canyon, I realized that getting back to Juarez that night was probably out of the question, and at the same time, my patience ran out. I couldn't sit there any longer doing nothing. I decided to go back up on the mountain in search of the cross. When I stood up to carry out my plan, I clearly heard God say, "They're coming." Just two simple words, but as God so often does, He did not tell me everything I wanted to know. He is not a tyrant. He always leaves us with a choice to follow His direction or to do things our own way. I needed to decide what I was going to do with what He gave me. There is an element of trust involved when God gives us information and direction. This is why He does not always show us the big picture. Was I going to trust Him and wait there for however long it was going to take for my rescuers to reach me? I wish I could tell you I was willing to trust Him while I waited for Him to move, but I can't. I failed miserably in the trust department. I desperately did not want to have to endure another cold night in the mountains, and because He did not tell me they were coming today, I set out following my own plan. I don't know if there were searchers heading in my direction at that moment, or if God spoke those words to encourage me and reaffirm my assurance of being rescued if not right away, then eventually.

Because I was unsure of where I had come down off the mountain the night before, I walked upstream until I found a place that was not so steep where I thought I could climb back up the mountain. After clawing my way up the steepest section on my hands and knees, I followed very narrow goat paths to the top. These paths were sometimes barely wider than my foot. I am sure there were angels watching over me and guiding my steps because I could have fallen many times. Psalm 91:11-12 says this about God's provision for us, "For He will command His angels concerning you to guard you in all your ways; they will lift you up in their hands so that you will not strike your foot against a stone" (NIV). I truly believe God had sent angels to watch over and support me as I navigated those very steep and slippery trails.

I roamed all over the top of the mountain searching for familiar landmarks, but I found none. Nor did I see or hear any evidence that anyone was out there searching for me. I felt totally alone, yet was still unafraid. When I was unsuccessful in finding the cross again, I knew I had to look for another way back down off the mountain. I found a ravine that looked like horses may have been taken down through it, so I decided to follow it. I tried to stay on horse trails as much as possible because I thought they might be looking for me on horseback, and I knew a horse trail would lead me off the edge of a cliff. This particular path was very steep and rocky. I twisted an ankle once and fell several times but suffered only small cuts to my hands to add to those I received when I was clawing my way up the side of the mountain. Before reaching the bottom, night fell once again. Earlier I had fought the prospect of spending another night out in the cold yet; here I was about to face the reality of it. Knowing that it was too dangerous to go any further in the dark, I spent the second night in that ravine among some rocks. Even though I knew what to expect as far as discomfort from the cold on this night, I was still unafraid. God is with us in the peace that He brings to us in the midst of the storm. Despite my desperately not wanting to be there, I had such peace, a peace that passes understanding, only because I knew God was with me.

Chapter Twenty-Two

WHAT'S YOUR STORY?

by Pastor Jorn

On the way back to Juarez, I (Jorn) had conversations with both Pastor Ron and Pastor Michael. When they asked what I was going to do, I told them I would not be leaving Mexico until we found LeAnn, dead or alive. If I had to stay two weeks or a month, I was committed to not leaving Mexico without her. For the sake of her mother and father, I had to do everything in my power to find LeAnn and to be there to deal with the situation. It would not have honored our commitments to people if I were to leave in the middle of this crisis. Pastor Michael, who was still in Texas, was making preparations to join me in Mexico as well. So I stayed and I would have stayed, no matter what.

When we arrived in Juarez, we unpacked and got settled in, again at the Bible Institute. I asked Kevin to take charge of getting the group back across the border after the Sunday evening church service. The plan was to spend Sunday night in a hotel in El Paso and catch our scheduled flight out the next morning.

A little later I was talking to Brenda when Kevin came in and

> **Larry** – "It was a long, quiet trip back to Juarez. When we got back there, we all got together and had a meeting, including praise and worship. Jorn gave us what you might call a pep talk. And from that time on, we were all reassured. It set something in me, and I just knew it was going to be okay, no matter what happened. I still hated having to leave, but I knew it was in the Lord's hands and everything would be okay. We decided that even though we only had a day or two left, we were going to make the best of the situation. We were scheduled to go to church the next day, and we were determined to go and praise the Lord with all we had."

84

said the group had been talking about the situation. Some had come to him with concerns about not having had visas and about the possibility they might be considered suspects in LeAnn's disappearance. They felt it would be best to leave Mexico immediately, rather than wait until the following evening as planned. It had been a long day, and we had already put a lot of pressure on the Mexican people who were our hosts. I did not want to make them pack everything up again so the group could go across the border because of fear. I decided I was not going to allow fear to dictate the group. So, I went to them and told them, in no uncertain terms, that they were staying where they were.

I told them we were going to follow our original plan for the rest of the trip. We had arranged for them to go shopping Sunday afternoon and to go to church that evening. After the church service, the Mexicans would take them back across the border to El Paso. I tried to reassure them that everything was going to be fine. I assured them there would be no problems, and they need not worry. I told them I had already talked to Brenda and Tomas, and they had explained that if there were any repercussions concerning the lack of visas, it would come back on them, never on us. I knew they would not tell us that just to make us feel better. That is not who they are. It's not part of their character. I knew they had never said anything untrue to me before, and I was confident I could trust them now.

Later that evening, we had worship together, and I shared with the group. I talked to them about the relationship LeAnn and I had shared over the last number of years. I told them my wife and I had had some very personal conversations with her about her life, about what Jesus meant to her, and about some of her own personal struggles. She had been transparent and had shared much of her life with me. I told them I knew beyond a shadow of doubt, that she has a quality relationship with God; she really trusts Jesus. I assured them they could rest in knowing that no matter what happened, LeAnn would say, "Listen, whether I am dead or alive, it is okay. I know who God is and He's my Savior." And I said, "I can tell you right now, if LeAnn were here, she would ask you why you want to turn back now?" She would say, "Stay, finish the trip, do everything you said you were going to do, and do it with all your strength, and with your whole heart." Because that's one thing we had talked about, giving your whole life away, not holding onto anything and being passionate to the very end. I let them know we still had hope that she was alive; so I challenged them to finish the trip as if she is alive, not as if she is gone. I wanted them to believe that things were going to be fine.

I reminded them that in every situation, they have the opportunity to glorify God and bring life in the middle of death. I told them that no matter what happens they have a story to tell. I asked them, "How are you going to tell that story? Are you going to tell a story about how Christ is Lord of our lives, and He divinely orchestrates and knows everything? Is your story going to be about overcoming adversity and fear, and giving people hope for the future no matter what happens? Or will it be a story of heartbreak, disillusionment, and hopelessness?"

We all have a story to tell, but in the end it has to bring glory to God. Whatever the circumstance, we have the opportunity to glorify God, even in tragedy. Job said a lot of things about the trials and struggles of his life, but in the end, he knew God was good and he wanted to glorify Him. We need to be like Job, bringing glory to God even in the difficult situations of our lives.

Chapter Twenty-Three

COMPANY OF ANGELS

by LeAnn

My decision to go back up on the mountain resulted in having to spend another night up there and ending up even further from my destination; but I knew that even though I had acted in my own flesh, God had not abandoned me. He did not let me do it alone. He did not remain where He had told me to stay, but instead, He followed after me. God placed a hedge of protection around me, and I was hidden in Him. I know the enemy would have liked nothing better than to have taken my life, but he couldn't touch me because I was in the shelter of the most high God. Looking back on this night, knowing now how many people were praying for me, I realize their prayers provided the covering I needed through the night. The prayers of my friends, my family, and God's people were like a warm blanket wrapped around me by God that night.

When I sat down among the rocks that night, I looked out across the ravine in front of me. I was surprised to see Davy sitting there. He took off his hat and scratched his head in a way that is so typical of him. Sam was sitting behind him and was speaking something over his shoulder. They both were laughing. Tom was with them too, welding helmet in his hand, and Shawn and Larry were there working on the steps. It was all so very real. I watched them for quite awhile. I even called out to them to see if they would answer me, but they did not. At the time, I thought I was hallucinating, or maybe even losing my mind. But as I have reflected on it since that time, I believe they were the angels God had sent to watch over me. Before I had gone on the trip, my mother was concerned about her single daughter going off to Mexico by herself, and I assured her I would have ten men, "protectors," to look after me. The angels revealed themselves as those I had considered protectors because that was their purpose, and they wanted me to feel safe. If they had revealed themselves in any other way it might have brought fear; so they chose to show themselves as people I trust. I had come to care about these men very much. Now, here they were visible before me, and I no longer felt alone.

I really did feel safe and did not have any fear, even though I desperately did not want to be out there. Some people have asked if I saw any wild animals, but I did not. I had not even seen a bug. I am sure I would not have been comfortable sitting there on the ground in the dark if I had seen any bugs sharing my space. The cold weather surely was a factor in this. Frigid air threatened to chill me to the bone; yet, at the same time protected me from seeing any insects that most certainly would have made the cold, dark night even more difficult than it was. I also knew I didn't have to worry about snakes because that was something I'd asked about before heading out into the mountains.

I tried to sleep that night so it would not seem so long, but the rocks were very hard compared to the one I had found the previous night. I could not find a comfortable position among the rocks. Part of the discomfort was because it was steep there. I felt a need to keep one foot braced against a rock in front of me to keep from tumbling down the ravine should I somehow manage to fall asleep. Because I was not able to sleep, the night again seemed endlessly long, and it was very cold. I shook uncontrollably throughout the night, praying as I waited for the first light of dawn. That night was even more difficult than the night before, but God was with me and again sustained me.

I was relieved when the sun finally came up, and I was able to continue down the ravine to the river. When I got there, I was disoriented and did not know which

Kent Knable (a member of Grace Covenant/Mt. Union) – "Our Sunday morning service was spent praying for LeAnn. As I listened to others praying, God had me pick up my Bible and He opened it to Ezekiel 34:11-16. It's a passage where God declares He's the shepherd and He's going after His sheep. He'll rescue them and bring them back from foreign lands. He will lead them on the mountains and beside the streams to places of rest. He will tend their wounds and strengthen them. As I read those words I had a very clear vision of LeAnn lying beside a stream near a ravine. God told me she was still alive and He was caring for her. I shared what I had seen and heard with the others. Then I began praying for LeAnn and that the rescuers would go to the stream near the ravine where I had seen her. This was still very strong in my spirit when my wife and I were driving home from church and I suggested that we should try to reach Jorn and tell him to look near the stream."

direction to go. I tried to remember which way the river flowed past the barn, but I just was not sure. I decided to go upstream and again came to a pool I could not get around. I was so desperate to get back to camp at this point, though, that I swam it without a second thought, even though I had seen ice along the edge of the river. I didn't bother to stop and wring out my clothes this time. I wanted to just keep moving, but the cold water quickly drained what little energy I had left. I soon began to get very tired and weak as I tried to step over and around the rocks along the riverbank. At one point, I sat down on a rock and quickly fell asleep in the warm sunshine. When I awoke, I got up to go on, but I found myself too weak to even stand, let alone walk. I was stopped in my tracks and sat down on a rock to wait, but for what, I was not sure. At that point I was probably closer to death than I had ever been in my life, and yet I didn't even consider that I might die, so strong was my faith that I would be rescued. I knew, though, that God was going to have to intervene because there was nothing more I could do. I was at the end of myself, now totally dependent on God for my rescue.

God is always with us in times of trouble. He is our rescuer. His Word says, "For the Son of Man came to seek and to save what was lost" (Luke 19:10 NIV). I was lost to the others, but God knew exactly where I was because He was there at the river with me.

Chapter Twenty-Four

SUNDAY MORNING

by Pastor Ron

From the moment I (Ron) got up on Sunday, my thoughts were with my congregation and the service we would be having that morning. Along with the maps I had gotten from the Internet the night before, I had also checked a weather site to find out how cold it had gotten in Juarez overnight. I was encouraged to see a low of forty degrees come up on my computer screen because I knew that was survivable. I took the things I had prepared and headed off to church with my family.

Wes came to me right before the service began. He said he was concerned about people's emotions because some of them were going to be hearing the news for the first time. Many of the church family were aware of what had happened, but still many others were not. He felt it was important to consider that as we started the service. I also knew I would be explaining the situation at the beginning of the service, so the focus would not be on God until later. Because of that, I knew there would be all kinds of thoughts going through their minds, which might cause them to struggle with their emotions. To combat those thoughts, I knew they were going to need prayer for themselves before they could pray with faith for LeAnn. I realized it was important to first deal with our own emotions and then with the emotions of those around us, because some would be able to handle their emotions better than others. I knew some of them would be crying, but I knew others would be okay.

After the worship team finished the first song, I got up and addressed the congregation. When I told them LeAnn was lost in Mexico, a few gasped. Then, as the news sank in, silence fell over the congregation and some started to cry quietly. I showed them the maps I had gotten from the Internet and told them of my research concerning the previous night's low temperature. I described what LeAnn had been wearing and assured them a low temperature of forty degrees was survivable. I tried to encourage them with all I knew about the efforts to find LeAnn as well. I then asked everyone to bow their heads and pray for themselves, asking God to calm their hearts while they focused on Him and His faithfulness. Next, I asked each one to take the hands of those next to them and pray for the person on their right and left. When they were through praying, I told them God knew exactly where LeAnn was at that moment, and it seemed to be a turning point for some of them. All of this was spontaneous. We hadn't preplanned any of it. Rather, the Spirit was leading us.

Wes was very important to the worship service that morning and to the support of the worship team of which LeAnn is a part. I knew those on the worship team were struggling as well, but they led us powerfully in worship. Emotion and anxiety could be heard in their voices in the beginning, but as the service went on, the anxiety in their voices was replaced with hope and victory.

Roberta encouraged the congregation to turn off their minds and tune in to the Holy Spirit. She talked about the importance of our prayers. She said, "God moves on the tracks of prayer that we lay down." She reminded the group that our God rules and reigns over all the earth, including the place where LeAnn was hidden. The blood of Jesus was over that place and evil could

Lee – "The next morning our phone started ringing. Many were calling to ask if what they heard was true or to let us know that they were praying for LeAnn's safe return. My brother took the phone calls unless someone specifically asked to speak with my wife or me. There was also a steady stream of visitors at our door and my sister brought enough food to feed them all. Family members and friends stopped by to encourage us and offer their support. That support was like a lifeline to us, and we were glad to be home and not back in Florida going through this crisis alone.

"There were also many calls from Pastor Ron and Cynthia at the consulate. They were such an encouragement to us. They called us every couple of hours whether they had any news or not.

"When LeAnn had left us in Florida a few weeks earlier, my wife's final words to her were, 'Don't let anyone take you when you are in Mexico.' We remembered those words when we were told of LeAnn's disappearance and feared that she had been abducted. We didn't have much hope for her survival and spent part of that afternoon talking about what kind of funeral service she would want us to have for her."

George Camp – "LeAnn is a worshiper and I believe she began to sing in her time of trouble. Psalm 40 says, "I waited patiently for the Lord; He turned to me and He heard my cry. He lifted me out of the slimy pit, out of the mud and mire; he set my feet on a rock and gave me a firm place to stand. He put a new song in my mouth, a hymn of praise to our God. Many will see and hear and put their trust in the Lord" (NIV).

Jackie Alters – Matthew 10:26 (NIV). "There is nothing concealed that will not be disclosed, or hidden that will not be made known."

Larry Shaffer – Psalm 27:5 and Psalm 28: 7-8. "For in the day of trouble He will keep me safe in His dwelling; He will hide me in the shelter of His tabernacle and set me high upon a rock. The Lord is my strength and my shield; my heart trusts in Him and I am helped. The Lord is the strength of His people, a fortress of salvation for His anointed one" (NIV).

not reign there.

Eva shared from Psalm 85 and prayed for the land of Rio Chico. She asked God to forgive the sins of the people of that land where false gods had been worshiped. She asked that the joy and life the team brought to that place would open the heavens and provide a channel for God's blessing to rain down on the land. She also talked about God's promise to always be our Good Shepherd. She told us that LeAnn was His precious lost sheep and He was reaching down to pick her up and return her to the fold.

Before giving opportunity for others to pray, I read a portion of Psalm 91 from the *Amplified Bible*, inserting LeAnn's name in the passage of scripture, which I felt held a prophetic message for her. "Because LeAnn has set her love upon Me, therefore will I deliver her; I will set her on high, because she knows and understands My name. She has a personal knowledge of My mercy, love, and kindness—trusts and relies on Me, knowing I will never forsake her, no, never. She shall call upon Me, and I will answer her; I will be with her in trouble, I will deliver her and honor her. With long life will I satisfy her and show her My salvation."

A foundation of faith had been laid, and many members of the congregation shared scriptures that came to their minds and prayed powerfully and in unity for LeAnn's restoration to the fold. I was very happy with the involvement of the other members of the congregation. It was a very emotional time. I thought many might be reluctant to pray because they were so overcome with emotion, but that wasn't the case. Many shared scriptures or prayed.

Sometime during that service I received a call from Jorn. He told me that again, they had searched all night and still had not found her. With him, I struggled with the question of why she had not heard them calling her name. I know Jorn is tenacious and would have searched everywhere, leaving no stone unturned. But if that were true, then I wondered why she would not have heard them. I never sensed in my own spirit that she was abducted, but I began to believe that she may have fallen and bumped her head. I thought this could be an explanation of why she had not heard their voices and responded. That was the one question that haunted me, *why didn't she hear them?*

To spare me further concern, Jorn had not told me how cold it was there. During our conversation that morning though, he mentioned something about ice. I said, "What do you mean, ice?"

> **Michael Bryan** – Isaiah 40:28-31 (NIV). "Do you not know? Have you not heard? The Lord is the everlasting God, the Creator of the ends of the earth. He will not grow tired or weary, and His understanding no one can fathom. He gives strength to the weary and increases the power of the weak. Even youths grow tired and weary, and young men stumble and fall; but those who hope in the Lord will renew their strength. They will soar on wings like eagles; they will run and not grow weary, they will walk and not be faint."

> **Dave Aurand** – "God has redeemed that moment when LeAnn chose to go in another direction. She is going through this for a reason and good is going to come out of it. If God chooses to move in a way such as this, we've got to get on board and go forward in Him. This situation won't deter us from going to Mexico; no, it's going to empower us to do even more. When LeAnn comes home, God will be glorified and we're going to love her and Jesus even more."

> **Eva, Sam's wife** – "No one spoke negative words during that Sunday service either. Of course there was some anxiety, but there was also faith in the house. Everyone had something to contribute to that service. It seemed like every time someone shared, it was the next step; each person built on the foundation that was laid by the last. The hope just kept building. When Dave Aurand spoke up and said the Lord showed him that even in the very moment LeAnn turned and went in the wrong direction, God had redeemed that. It was under the blood and it was no more a wrong direction because God had taken control over this whole situation and changed its direction. I think that was the turning point for me. It just all came together like pieces of a puzzle and by the end of the service there was a sense that LeAnn was with the Shepherd."

He said, "Ron, there's ice on the puddles." I told him I had checked the Internet and it showed a low of 40 degrees. Jorn said, "No, it's in the 20s here at night." All I could respond with was, "Oh, my goodness," and he said, "Yes, it's cold." I did not share that bit of information with the congregation, but in my heart I knew she couldn't survive another night in those conditions.

Our prayers were joined with the prayers of literally thousands of people around the country and around the world that morning. The churches in "Big Valley" were praying. The pastors at the ministers' conference were praying. Those at the International House of Prayer were praying. Anita's church and LeAnn's co-workers in Lancaster County were praying. From Pennsylvania, to North Carolina, Texas, Missouri, and Hawaii, churches were praying, but there were also churches praying in Argentina, Liberia, Nigeria, and Haiti. The global church had come together in faith believing for LeAnn's rescue.

The service that morning was very unique. There was a special spirit there, like nothing I had ever experienced before. There was a lot of faith in the house that day. I get chills just thinking about the level of faith and the unity that was there. It was powerful. We were unified in faith like we have never been before. So many people left that service knowing LeAnn would be found. They prayed, they believed, and that was it. It was done, and that sense was widespread.

At the end of the service I told everyone I was expecting a call from the consulate at 2:30 p.m. and that I would know nothing more until then. I asked that they give my ears a break and not call. I assured them that if we heard anything, we would get word to them. As they left, I asked them to continue to pray the Word of God in faith, believing in God's faithfulness and for LeAnn's rescue.

There was a powerful presence of God in that service, but because He is God, He could also be with LeAnn and the team in Mexico and in those churches all over the country and the world as His people gathered together in unity of purpose.

Candace Rager – Philippians 4:4-7 (NIV) "Rejoice in the Lord always. I will say it again: Rejoice! Let your gentleness be evident to all. The Lord is near. Do not be anxious about anything, but in everything, by prayer and petition, with thanksgiving, present your requests to God. And the peace of God, which transcends all understanding, will guard your hearts and your minds in Christ Jesus."

Chapter Twenty-Five

COMING TOGETHER

by Pastor Jorn

Davy – "Saturday night was terrible. We were at the Bible Institute and it was so cold in that room, it was unreal. I went out into the hallway and fired up a couple of propane heaters and slept there, in front of the heaters, where it was a bit warmer. It was still dark when I was awakened by a knock on the door. Brenda popped her head in and asked were Jorn was. I said, 'Close the door, its cold outside!' Jorn was exhausted when he went to bed and had overslept. I woke him and handed him the clothes Brenda had washed for him. As soon as he was dressed, he and Brenda headed back to Rio Chico."

Very early Sunday morning, Brenda and I (Jorn) left Juarez to go back to Rio Chico. Brenda was the one I always communicated with when planning our trips to Mexico. She was very careful how she talked to me, though, because she didn't know me personally. During that six-hour trip back to Rio Chico, we had the opportunity to talk about a lot of things. We were getting to know each other much better because we were going through this crisis together. At one point in our journey, I asked her what she thought of LeAnn's chances. She said, "Jorn, we can always hope, but there is a pretty good chance LeAnn's dead, that we're not going to find her alive." She thought LeAnn may not have been able to survive those two very cold nights because she was inadequately dressed. That time together, along with the thoughts and feelings we shared during the trip, really strengthened our relationship. It will never be the same because of what we went through together.

Back in Juarez, the team gathered to have their own church service. Denny opened with prayer and Josh led worship, which was described as very powerful. José Manuel, a student at the Bible Institute, joined them. Ben spoke on God's power, and he said the team could trust God to bring a victorious end to our crisis.

When Brenda and I got back to Rio Chico, we found the search still going strong. Pastor Ron had called the United States Consulate and the military had been sent to aid in the search. There were also police officers from Madera and another nearby town. In addition to the official searchers, there were many people from all over the area who had come to offer their help. I was amazed at the number of people who had come to help us in our time of need. By lunchtime, there were people everywhere. There were basically three groups: the military, the police, and local citizens. They planned their strategy together, and then broke up into groups to continue the search. Many of the locals were amazed to see the different arms of the government working together. They said that was highly unusual, and I knew that it was God who brought all these people together and put in them a concern for an American woman they'd never met.

There were a lot of men out searching, but one thing the Lord showed me that day was that we can never put our hope in men. Our hope has to be in God and God alone. Juan, Tomas' brother,

Diane – "While Ben was speaking; I had a very clear picture of LeAnn with brightness all around her. I felt the brightness represented warmth for LeAnn's body, the warmth of God's love. I also saw a Hispanic, dark chocolate colored, man's hand reaching for LeAnn's hand. It was a hand that had known hard work, rough and callused. I realized Jesus' hand must have looked much like that. He would have been dark skinned and His work as a carpenter would have caused his hands to be rough and callused. I saw the dark callused hand take LeAnn's pale delicate hand in his. I believed that hand was Ramon's or the hand of Jesus. I knew then that LeAnn would be ok. I did not know how or when, but I believed that Ramon would have some role in LeAnn's rescue.

I decided to add action to my faith that afternoon when we went shopping. Realizing LeAnn may not have a chance to do any shopping before going home, I decided to purchase something for her. I found a beautiful angel carved from native wood that I planned to present to her when she got home."

came to me and told me he had found three footprints in a cave the night be-fore. He wanted to take me there so I could look at them. He, Antonio, one of the trackers, and I took one of the trucks as far as we could. Then we had to hike a long, steep, winding path down to the cave where Juan had found the footprints. I went in the cave and inspected the footprints, but immediately, I knew LeAnn had not left them. The prints were large and left by someone wearing hiking boots. I believed LeAnn had been wearing sneakers and knew her feet were smaller than the footprints. Then we walked further down the mountain to a dry creek bed leading into the Rio Chico. If we had followed it around the mountain, eventually we would have come to the river. It was all the way over on the other side of the mountain from camp. We spent some time searching for other footprints, but Antonio couldn't find anything, so we decided to head back to camp.

As we hiked up the mountain, Juan was trying to console and encourage me with other ideas for finding LeAnn. I was frustrated though, and I just wanted to be left alone. We were about three quarters of the way back up the path when I told Juan and Antonio that I was tired and needed to sit down for a while. I sat down on a rock and asked the others to please go back to the truck and leave me alone for a few minutes. I wasn't doing very well emotion-ally at that moment. I was thinking about the possibility of having to call LeAnn's parents to tell them she was gone. I thought about having to escort her body home in a casket, and I was imagining how difficult it would be to stand in front of her family, friends, and the church to preach at her funeral. I was pouring my heart out to God as I sat there. I wanted to find her so badly and was feeling helpless and frustrated by the unsuccessful search efforts. I said, "God, I just want to find her! I don't know where she is, but You do. Please show me where she is."

I had screamed LeAnn's name hundreds of times over the last three days hoping she would hear my voice. As I was sitting there though, I got a revela-tion. I asked myself, "Why am I yelling her name when apparently she can't hear it?" I then stood up and instead of screaming LeAnn's name; I started screaming the name of Jesus as loudly as I could. I yelled "JESUS!" over and over again. After awhile, I turned and continued up the path to the truck. On the way there, something happened inside me. I came to a point of surrender or release. I said to myself, "Okay fine, if she's dead, she's dead; and there's nothing I can do about it." I suddenly sensed the Lordship of God in our situ-ation and in that moment, I said, "God, I can get all bent out of shape about this, but there's nothing more I can do. You know where she is and if she's alive or not, and I release her to you."

When I got back to the truck, Juan continued his efforts to console me and offer suggestions for what we could do next to try to find LeAnn, but I had had enough. I looked at him and said, "I want to tell you something and I want you to listen to me. My hope isn't in you or any other man out here. I have no hope in you or any of the other men who are searching because if LeAnn were to be found by the efforts of men, she would already have been found. We have done all we could possibly do and have not been able to find her." I said, "My hope now is in God and God alone. Only God can help us find her. It's apparent that we are not going to be able to do it on our own, or we would already have found her." With that, he started up the truck and nothing more was said as we headed back to camp.

Chapter Twenty-Six

IT'S UP TO YOU

by Pastor Ron

I (Ron) spent most of that afternoon praying. Not being able to sit still, I roamed all over the house praying. From the upstairs, to the basement, I prayed. As promised and right on time at 2:30, Cynthia called me again, even though she had nothing new to tell me. She was very good about keeping in touch and was always true to her word.

There was a point, late that afternoon, when I was getting really desperate. It was around 5:30 in the evening, 3:30 in Mexico; and this time, I was praying in my bedroom. I was thinking about what Jorn had said that morning about how cold it had been there. I knew if there was ice on the puddles, it had to have been at least 28 or 30 degrees. I also knew there was no way LeAnn was going to be able to continue to survive in that kind of weather. I knew she probably had not had anything to eat and in the cold weather you have to eat to stay warm. I sensed if she had to stay out there another night, she would probably not survive it. I was not even aware at the time, of her other physical challenges with diabetes and hypothyroidism, but I knew exposure alone would kill her if she was not found soon.

In desperation I cried out to God. I said, "God, either You are going to cause her to be found, or she's going to die. God, You've got to make this happen and NOW!" Then the Lord spoke to me and assured me that LeAnn had been found. What amazes me about God is that He knows what we need to hear. I needed to hear that because I was desperate. I did not want to have to face the congregation and tell them LeAnn was no longer alive. I especially didn't want to have to call her parents to break the news to them. I cried out to God and He heard my cry. The first thing I did was to go downstairs and tell my wife what had happened, because I knew that it was important. When God speaks to us, we need to verbalize it, speak it forth and tell someone. So I went down and said to my wife, "Cyndi, the Lord just told me that LeAnn has been found."

God is with us in that still small voice, and He's faithful to answer when we cry out to Him. I'm so grateful for the voice of God, and I really needed to hear His voice that afternoon. He will speak if we will only learn to listen.

Bonnie, Jorn's wife – "I was praying for LeAnn on Sunday afternoon when God told me LeAnn had been found and my husband would be calling me soon with the news. From that point on, I was at peace and knew it was finished; our crisis was over."

Chapter Twenty-Seven

WAS LOST BUT FOUND

by LeAnn

Back at the river, it did not seem very long before I looked up and saw men coming down the mountain from all directions. I had expected to be found by someone I recognized, but these men were unfamiliar to me. I somehow realized they were military and were looking for me. I must have been drifting in and out of consciousness because I do not remember seeing them walking up to me; but suddenly they were there next to me, and I was very relieved. We could not communicate well, but they were all very kind. They asked in Spanish if I could walk, and I told them I could not. They helped me across the river and sat me down on the other side. I remember thinking that they looked awfully young to have been sent on this mission, but I can remember nothing else about what they looked like. I can't picture their faces at all, but wish so much that I could.

I was not aware of it, but they used their radios to let those back at camp know that I had been found. They told them that my clothes were wet and asked that someone bring dry clothes for me. I was aware of them shooting their rifles two times and thought that was their signal to those back at camp that I had been found. I remember thinking, *the code must have been one if dead and two if alive.* In reality though, it was a signal for Juan, who was driving one of the trucks out on an old road. He used the sound of the rifle fire to determine our location and to get as close as possible. One of them took off my shoes and socks and wrapped my feet in bandages while another knelt next to my head and stroked my face saying, "No, no, no" each time I started to fall asleep or lose consciousness, I'm not sure which. They did not know at this point what condition I was in. Was I in shock? How much damage had been done to my body from exposure to the cold? I wanted to rest, but he was merely trying to prevent me from slipping into unconsciousness for fear I would not come out of it.

I only remember bits and pieces of the time we spent there by the river. I was aware that they had started cutting off my jeans and took off my wet sweatshirt. I was amazed to see they had the sweatpants and sweatshirt I had been sleeping in all week, but I was too weak to try to figure out how it came to be that these five guys somehow had my clothes. Before they got the jeans off and the other clothes on me though, I was out again. Months later, when Pastor Tomas and Brenda came to Pennsylvania, they explained to me the reason for the gun shots and the fact that the military had my clothes was that Ramon had brought them out to where I was, but I had not even realized Ramon was there. I thought they took me to the other side of the river, shot their rifles, and changed my clothes rather quickly, but Brenda told me this all happened over a span of two hours. That came as quite a shock to me because I thought we were by the river for just a short time.

I was told they formed a stretcher out of their coats and began to carry me up out of the canyon. I lost consciousness again or fell asleep because I don't remember any of that. It's probably best though because I would have agonized over their having to carry me, especially when I was told later that it was a couple hour trek out of the canyon. I thought that explained why it was already dark when we got up to the road. Jorn told me later, though that it wasn't dark at all, the sun did not set for another hour or so. The darkness must have been attributed to my semi-conscious state. The truck Juan had driven down the old road to meet the military guys and me had been prepared with a mattress and many Indian blankets to warm my body. When they put me in the back of the truck, I awoke to see the faces of Ramon and Rosenda beside me, but everything else was darkness. The only things I saw beyond their faces were dark shapes that must have been my rescuers. It warmed my heart more than any blanket could, to have them there with me. It was wonderful to see their familiar faces and the love and concern they had for me. They had known me less than a week, and we hadn't even been able to communicate that much. Yet there was a connection there that was from God, and I was so grateful to all of them.

I can't begin to express how wonderful it was to finally see the familiar faces of Ramon and Rosenda after the many long hours of being alone in the wilderness. I felt their love as they cared for me in the back of that truck. God is with us in the love He sends to us through the caring and heartfelt compassion of others He brings into our lives. He calls us to spread His love to those around us as well.

Chapter Twenty-Eight

DAY TO CELEBRATE

by Pastor Jorn

When we arrived back at camp and pulled into the gate, we were met by a woman who told us LeAnn had been found. She had a smile on her face, but I (Jorn) had to be sure, so I asked the question, "Dead or alive?" She said, "Alive, she's alive. She's okay." The military men had found her, and it was only 15 minutes after I had been screaming the name of Jesus at the top of my lungs instead of LeAnn's name.

Juan and I were ecstatic. We were yelling and giving each other high-fives. The heavy burden we'd been carrying for LeAnn was finally lifted from our shoulders. We were told that the military had found her along the river on the other side of the mountain. They had radioed back to camp and said her clothes were wet and asked that some dry clothes be brought out for her. Ramon was already on his way out with a pair of sweat pants and a sweatshirt. The military said she was in a very steep canyon, and they were going to have to make a stretcher on which to carry her out. At camp they were making preparations to drive one of the trucks out an old road to get as close as possible to where she was. Knowing there was nothing more I could do there and anxious to see for myself that LeAnn was okay, I started running down along the river in the direction I knew them to be. I decided I would just keep following the river until I came to the place where she was with the military guys. I kept going and going, expecting to find her around the next bend. I rounded many such bends in the river and still had not found them. I thought, *Oh, my gosh, she must be way down there.* I could not imagine how she had gotten so far away from camp. A couple of times I looked up at the sheer cliffs lining the river bank and thought, *My God, if she had fallen from one of those cliffs, she would have killed herself.* Finally I came to an area that I couldn't get through and would have to climb the riverbank to find a way around. At that point I had to tell myself that the military men were taking care of her. I knew that if I allowed my wrung out emotions to control my actions, I would risk getting lost myself. So I just turned around and returned to camp.

When I got there, I retrieved the satellite phone and went up on another mountain to call the church where the team would be worshiping that evening. Worship was just getting started when Shawn answered the phone. The music was loud in the background, but he was able to hear me tell him LeAnn had been found and that she was okay. He started screaming, "She's alive, she's alive!" and mass hysteria broke out in that place. Everyone was shouting, laughing, and crying, all at the same time. As I listened to my team members shouting, celebrating, and praising God, a smile spread across my face. I was remembering the hard decision I had to make when I insisted they stay in Mexico and finish the trip as planned. I knew that decision was a correct one and I was glad, because otherwise they would have missed this opportunity to celebrate God's goodness to us with the Mexican people. Most of them will tell you that church service was

> **Josh (Pastor Danny's son)** – "The service was just getting started and I was standing next to Maria Bencomo when her cell phone rang. The person on the other end of the call was speaking Spanish, but I thought they said LeAnn was found. I wasn't sure, but I immediately called my Dad. Minutes later, Pastor Jorn called and verified the report. What a time of celebration! The worship was good at the beginning, but the place really started to rock after we got the news. We had a lot to praise God for!"

> **Davy** – "At the end of the service, the pastor told us to pray with each other. An older Mexican woman came up to me, laid her hand on my shoulder, and began praying for me. As she prayed, I felt a warmth come over my body. I don't know if she was praying in Spanish or some other tongue, but in my spirit I knew what she was saying. I also knew that she had a connection with God because what she said was very personal and was what I needed at the time. I prayed for her as well and I believe that she too understood my words as our spirits connected and tears streamed down both our faces. We both sensed that we were experiencing some deep things of God. Later she folded her arms in front of her chest as if holding a baby and said the name, Gonzalo. We realized then that this must be Gonzalo's mother, the man who had joined us in our frantic search when he returned from his mission to the canyon."

probably the most powerful worship experience of their lives. Even though they couldn't understand the language, the presence of God was just so heavy in that place. And they would have missed it all if they had crossed the border the night before.

It came as quite a surprise to the military and others who were looking for LeAnn to find her alive. None of them thought she was alive. They all thought they were looking for her body. They were convinced she had probably died of exposure because those two nights had been so cold. For me, I know it was a supernatural thing that she was found alive. There is no way she should have survived for two nights out there as cold as it was and being diabetic. But we, who are in Christ, believe that Jesus raised the dead. On Friday, LeAnn went into the grave, but oh, for Sunday when she came out!

Chapter Twenty-Nine

GIVING THANKS

by Pastor Ron

An hour after I (Ron) received the word from the Lord that LeAnn had been found; I got a call from my brother Danny. He told me his son, Josh, had called him from Juarez and told him LeAnn had been found. Concerned that they could have misunderstood or gotten a false report in Juarez, I was a bit skeptical not having heard from Jorn. While I was on the phone with Danny, my other phone rang, and it was the woman from Neffsville that I had talked to the day before. She told me her church had been praying for LeAnn's safe return, and she wanted to know if we had heard any news. I told her I was at that moment getting a preliminary report of her rescue, and that I would have to call her back. She said, "Praise God" and let me get back to my conversation with Danny. When I got off the phone with Danny, I called his son in Juarez and heard the celebration that was going on in the church service there, but I still wanted to hear it from Jorn.

Lee – "At around 6:00 that evening, my son and his family arrived. They had not told their sons, Josiah and Gabriel, much about what was happening and the boys were hanging on every word as the rest of us discussed the situation. Just before we were to sit down to dinner together, I breathed a prayer saying, "God, I don't know how I am going to sit down at this table without LeAnn." A few minutes later, when my son was asking the blessing, we got that first call from Pastor Ron, telling us that he thought LeAnn had been found. The phone rang again about ten minutes later, and my brother handed me the phone. Pastor Ron told me LeAnn had indeed been found, and she was ok. When I got off the phone, my brother suggested we pray again and we did, thanking God for his faithfulness to our family. Later, Gabriel, my nine-year-old grandson, was the first to suggest that his 'Tia Annie' needed to write a book."

I then called LeAnn's family and told them that I thought LeAnn had been found, but it had not yet been confirmed. A little later, I was again praying, this time in our breakfast nook when Jorn called. When he told me LeAnn was found and was okay, I lost it. All the emotion that had been building in me was finally released. I didn't cry earlier when Danny called, but when Jorn called, that was it. I knew it was over! I sat there and cried for ten or fifteen minutes.

Chapter Thirty

MEXICAN HOSPITAL

by LeAnn

Somewhere along the old mountain road was an ambulance waiting to take me to a hospital. I was aware of a cheering crowd of well wishers when they transferred me from the truck to the ambulance, but I couldn't see them. Immediately, Juan joined me in the back of the ambulance. He kissed my forehead and said, "I'm so glad you are okay," then he took one of my very cold hands in his. I thought Jorn jumped in right after Juan, but he told me he had run up the highway from camp where the ambulance picked him up a little later. When he joined me, his actions mirrored Juan's. He said, "I'm so glad you are okay," kissed my forehead, and took the other hand. I was not aware of how sick I was and didn't think I needed to go to the hospital, but I was not about to argue with Jorn about it after all the trouble I had already caused. I was happy to put myself into his very capable hands, and I couldn't have had more attentive caregivers. It was wonderful to see them and to finally have someone I could communicate with in English. I guess I took advantage of that because Jorn later told me I talked the whole way to the hospital. I don't remember much of the

> **Pastor Ron** – "The most frustrating thing for me was not being able to be in constant contact with Jorn. The satellite phone didn't always work, and he didn't always have cell reception or his phone needed recharging. There were times when we'd finally be able to connect only to be cut off after a few seconds. I was able to reach him at one point on Sunday afternoon, and he told me they were in the ambulance on the way to the hospital. He couldn't talk long at that time, but he was good about calling me when he could. He called me later from the hospital to update me on LeAnn's condition and assured me she was doing well."

conversation though. Jorn said I was a bit delirious. The one thing I do remember was telling Jorn how sorry I was for all the trouble I had caused. I know how much he loves to preach the Word, and he had been scheduled to preach in four separate services that day. Like the Good Shepherd, he had left his plans and the others behind to find his one lost sheep. I don't remember the ambulance or the attendant, but Jorn described the ambulance as an old van with homemade benches built into it. He said there were bottles rolling across the floor, and he found it odd that the driver was wearing rubber gloves, yet he did not seem to be concerned about the bottles on the floor.

> **Lee** – "Later that evening, Pastor Jorn called us from the hospital. He told us that LeAnn was being treated for hypothermia and dehydration. We asked if we could talk to her, but he said the doctor was with her and she was very tired. He told us he would have LeAnn call us in the morning, after she'd had a chance to get some rest."

They took me to a clinic which was very nice and clean, probably the best Madera had to offer. They put me in a spacious room with a bed on one side and a sitting area on the other. While I cannot be sure, I believe I may have been the only patient in the clinic at the time. The nurse helped me out of my sweats and into a hospital gown while Jorn and Juan admitted me. As soon as I was in bed, the guys returned to rub my feet in an effort to warm my very cold toes. Pastor Tomas, Brenda and Gonzalo soon joined our little gathering. Brenda found me some soup, but my throat was too sore to swallow more than a few bites. I am sure it was sore from both the exposure to the cold as well as all the screaming I had done.

The doctor was very kind as were his nurses, but they did not speak English. I was dependant on Juan and Brenda to do my communicating for me. I had not been a hospital patient since my birth, and I thought it very ironic that my first hospital stay since then would happen in Mexico. After everyone left me to get some sleep, the nurse set a bell by my bedside to ring during the night should I need her help. Before I fell asleep, a man walked into my room and began talking to me. I had no idea who he was and I told him I was sorry, but I could not understand what he was saying. He seemed disappointed not to be able to communicate with me, and I felt badly about that. He left a card and wrote a personal note on the back that said, "With affection, it is good that you are well. I worried about your health. May God take care of you many more years." The next morning Brenda told me that the person who left the card was the municipal president!

I am sure I do not need to explain why seasoned travelers tell you not to drink the water in Mexico. Most everyone has heard about the problems that ensue when you do. During the night, the after affects of drinking the river water hit. I needed to get to the bathroom, but no matter how hard I rang the bell or how loudly I called out, I could not get any help. I could not reach the bathroom on my own because I was connected to an IV. I realized that for the first time in my life, I was going to have to use a bedpan. But only after I was finished did I realize the nurse had failed to leave any toilet paper for me. I did the best I could with what I had to clean up, put the bedpan on the floor, and crawled back in bed. What else could I do? The nurse came back in my room a few minutes later. Thankfully, she took the bedpan off to the bathroom and brought me some toilet paper. It was a little too late, but I thanked her, and she left me to get some more rest and fluids.

She was back in a few minutes with the doctor who added some medication to my IV, which was supposed to take care of my illness. Unfortunately, it did not start working immediately. An hour or so later, I had to go to the bathroom once again. This time I had toilet paper, but now, I had no bedpan. The nurse had left it in the bathroom! I rang the bell again and yelled, but as before, neither produced a response. I finally got out of bed and managed to reach a chair on the other side of the room which I pulled over to the bed. I crawled up on the chair to unhook the IV bottle from the ceiling. Then, I carried the IV bottle to the bathroom with me. When I was finished in the bathroom, I returned to the chair, hung the IV back up, and got back in bed.

> **LeAnn** – When I related this story to the members of our mission team months later, Davy leaned around those seated between us so he could look me in the face and ask, "Did you use your underwear?" I was laughing so hard all I could do was nod my head in answer to his question. He responded confidently, "That's what I'd a done!"

I did not sleep well that night. I realized that I could hear my heartbeat in my ear when I laid on it which only happens when my thyroid is working overtime. I believe God must have touched my thyroid to increase my metabolism so that I could withstand the cold. Normally, someone who has hypothyroidism, like me, is very sensitive to cold. In addition to the thyroid disorder, I am also diabetic. Being out in the cold, with no food or water for all that time could have spelled disaster, yet my body managed to cope without medication. This was clearly one of the many provisions that God blessed me with while I was lost.

The next morning I was very surprised and happy to get a phone call from my family. It was wonderful to speak with all of them, especially the boys. I was sure they had been very worried about me. I assured them that, with the exception of some minor cuts, sore fingers and toes, I was fine.

The doctor came in a little later that morning and asked me in broken English, "You want go home today?" I answered a resounding, "YES!" It was not long after that when Jorn and Brenda came to take me "home" to Rio Chico. Jorn sat down on the couch and said, "Look what I've brought you!" He pulled out socks, jeans, sweatshirt, underwear, and shoes. He even had my makeup bag, curling iron and hairdryer, but I realized there was no bra. When I asked about it, his face fell, and he let out a frustrated, "Ugh!" He was trying so hard to take good care of me and was disappointed that he had forgotten this one detail. But, to me, this was just a minor thing compared to all he had already done for me. He told me I was not going to be able to wear my dress shoes over my sore toes anyway, so he would go out and buy me some sneakers and a bra. He really did go the extra mile! I will always be grateful for his loving kindness.

While he and Brenda were out buying my clothing items and something for me to eat, I was able to take a hot shower. I was beginning to feel human again, but I quickly discovered that just showering and getting dressed exhausted me. I was still very weak. While I was resting and waiting for Jorn and Brenda to return, a woman came into my room and asked if she could interview me for the radio. At first I refused, telling her I would not understand, but she assured me it would work out fine. She came back into the room with a guy who spoke English and could interpret for me, so I consented. They asked who I was, where I was from, and what I was doing there. I explained that I was with a group from my church, and we were doing work for Pastor Tomas who has a ministry to the Indians in the Copper Canyon.

Jorn walked into the room as our interview was ending. I thought it odd that he immediately turned and left. When the people from the radio station left, he returned and brought with him breakfast, the first solid food I had had since lunch on Friday. A sausage, egg, and cheese burrito never tasted so good! I asked Jorn how I was going to pay for my treatment. He assured me that he had already taken care of it. The bill was for a little over 6,000 pesos, around

$600. Jorn had taken the money out of an account he had set up for the trip and told me that all I would need to do was reimburse Pastor Tomas when I got home. I was so grateful to have him take charge and care for my needs because I was struggling to just put one foot in front of the other at that point.

We made a couple of stops in and around Madera before returning to camp. By the time we finished with lunch, I was ready for a nap. Jorn moved all my belongings into a room next to his and made sure there were plenty of blankets on the bed. Those wonderful Indian blankets were like friends to us. He said he moved me to that room because the bed was better, but it may have been because the wall between us was thin, and he would be able to hear me if I needed anything during the night, unlike my nurses the night before. He really was an excellent caregiver, concerned about every aspect of my health—physical, emotional and spiritual.

When I got up, Juan made sure there was a roaring fire going in the fireplace in the dining room. I mentioned to him that my fingertips still felt very cold to the touch. He looked at them and told me they were frostbitten. My doctor may have mentioned frostbite, but if he did, I had not understood him. I thought the soreness in my fingers and toes came from all the mountain climbing I had done, but Juan said no, I had frostbite to blame for that discomfort. So I stretched my feet and hands toward the fire, and I made myself comfortable there until dinner. As I stared at the flames, enjoying their warmth, I was reflecting on all that had happened over the last few days and was overwhelmed by God's goodness and His faithfulness to me. I was also touched by all the love and care shown me by those at camp and was very grateful for the opportunity to go back there to rest, recuperate, and soak up the peace and serenity of that place.

Jorn, Juan, and Brenda made sure I had everything I needed to rest and regain my strength. God does that too. He is with us as He cares for and watches over us, supplying all we need for life and godliness.

Chapter Thirty-One

ANOTHER IS RESCUED

by Pastor Jorn

Through this experience, God taught me that, no matter what is going on, God's heart is always for people, all people. His heart was toward LeAnn, but at the same time, His heart was for all the people who were searching for her, all the Mexicans we were ministering to, and all those back home who were praying. God's heart was turned toward everyone who was crying out to Him, everyone at the same time. He also cared about those who didn't know Him.

While LeAnn was sleeping the afternoon after we had brought her back from the hospital, someone mentioned to me that Christian was not a Christian. He was 28 years old with a wife and three children back in Juarez, but he didn't know Christ. I (Jorn) decided to go out to the barn to talk to him. I found him there and asked him, "How can you have the name Christian and not be a Christian?" He just kind of shrugged his shoulders and said he didn't know. I just kept asking, "Why, why wouldn't you want to give your life to God? He loves you." Christian just stood there looking at me kind of starry-eyed, and he didn't answer me. He may not have completely understood what I was saying. Using gestures and my limited Spanish vocabulary, I explained to him that I wanted to sit down with him that evening and talk to him about God. I told him I wanted to show him something in the Bible, and he said that would be okay.

I left him in the barn and walked up to the cross. This was my third trip to Rio Chico, yet I had never been up there. I decided to go up to the cross and spend some time with the Lord, reading my Bible. I wanted to sit there, by the cross, and meditate on the things that God had done. While there, my heart was stirred for Christian, down in the barn below me. As I prayed for him, I said, "Lord, I sure would like to lead him to Jesus. I would really like to have the opportunity to share Christ with him." And I asked the Lord if He would give me a word of knowledge; tell me something about Christian's life that no one else would know except Him. After a few moments, the Lord spoke to me very clearly about Christian's life. I hid the word from the Lord in my heart and prayed over it.

As I continued to pray for Christian, I thought about how he had responded to our crisis even though he was not a fellow believer. When Christian found out LeAnn was lost, he left immediately. He was the first one to go out looking for her, and he literally ran up the side of the mountain. He searched everywhere and he continued searching until 2:00 the next morning. I had made my team come in at midnight, but Christian was still out looking for LeAnn. At the crack of dawn the next day he went out again. He searched the whole day until 4:00 the following morning. I marveled at the concern shown

> **Pastor Ron** – "I managed to get in touch with Jorn again and told him that we wanted to have a celebration during our Wednesday evening service. That would mean they would need to leave Rio Chico the next day in order to get back in time. Jorn said he would have preferred to give LeAnn another day to rest, but they decided they would try to be home in time, so I booked their flights for Wednesday morning."

and the effort put forth by this man who didn't know Jesus. There were other men there who knew Christ, who had come in early, but he stayed out late and he was the one that didn't know God.

After dinner, LeAnn and I shared a devotional time with Pastor Tomas and the others from camp who had searched so tirelessly for her. Pastor Tomas said the scriptures were an encouragement to him during those days of tribulation. He said they all joined in the battle with me, and they all were sharing in the joy of the victory. He talked about the love and concern shown by the non-Christians in the area. He said even they shared our joy. He encouraged those living at the camp to do all they could to maintain their connection with the local people who walked with us through our crisis. He shared that in Psalm 102, God taught David that his pain would be forgotten when God shows up. We would forget the heartache, but we would never forget the great things He had done here over the last few days. He said many did not think we would find LeAnn alive, but God showed them that He is still a miracle working God!

Then I told them that I had been considering all my reasons for wanting to continue coming to Rio Chico. With my upcoming talk with Christian in the back of my mind, I shared with them that for five years I was involved in a

> **LeAnn** – "Pastor Tomas gave me a chance to speak, and I struggled to find words that would adequately express my gratitude to them and to God. I tried to tell them how very much I appreciated all their love and concern and thanked them all for their efforts to find me. I also thanked them for their prayers and expressed my gratefulness to God for sparing my life. It was all very overwhelming."

prison ministry. For three of those years, I went to the prison alone. The prisoners did not understand why I would do that for them, but it was because I loved them. I told those gathered in the dining room that evening that I felt the same conviction about going to Rio Chico. I shared with them that when I saw the love and concern on the faces of the people there when we were in the midst of our crisis, I saw the love of God. I told them that the Indians in the canyon need many things, but the thing they need most is someone to love them. I encouraged the group to live lives of integrity, because without it our witness is tainted. Titus 2:7 says, "But mostly, show them all this by doing it yourself, incorruptible in your teaching, your words solid and sane." I said our actions speak louder than words. People who don't know God see our actions and ask themselves what's different about us that would cause us to do the things we do. They will want to find out what is behind our actions and will be drawn to Jesus in us, as we live lives that reflect His love.

Pastor Tomas then gave others an opportunity to share thoughts concerning the events of the last few days. Gilberto, Ramon's son, said he had not thought that LeAnn would be found alive, but he was giving thanks for the miracle God provided. Ramon also gave God praise for sparing LeAnn's life. With tears in her eyes, Rosenda said she was beginning to lose hope for LeAnn's survival and was grateful to God for His protection over her. Gabby said he was not able to go out looking for LeAnn, but realized his role was to stay behind and pray. He was providing a vital prayer covering for LeAnn, as well as for the searchers, as he paced up and down the road. Pastor Tomas said his only prayer was that LeAnn would be returned safely to them.

When we finished our devotional time, I asked Christian to join Brenda and me in the kitchen. Brenda interpreted for us. I began to share with him how thankful I was for him and how much I appreciated his concern for LeAnn and his desire to see her rescued. I said to him, "You know, God wants to rescue you. The same way you searched for LeAnn, He's searching for you and He loves you so much." I then began to share with him the word God had given me, that his father had abandoned him when he was little, and he had never had a good role model. He never had anyone to show him who God really is, because his father was never there to be that example to him. He began to cry and tears ran down his face. He cried the whole time I was talking to him. I shared the love of Christ with him and asked him if he would want to give his life to Jesus. He nodded and quietly said he would. With his eyes full of tears, he prayed to receive Christ as his Savior. He went to bed with tears in his eyes that night because Jesus searches for everyone. He does that because He loves us. He reaches out to each one of us and will touch our lives with His love if we will only allow Him to. No matter what's happening, God's heart is always to win the lost. It's His desire to use any opportunity and every crisis to win people to Jesus.

God was with us in the power He displayed in sparing LeAnn's life, but also in the new life experienced by Christian that night, one life saved and another life changed.

Chapter Thirty-Two

ONE FINAL WISH

by LeAnn

I don't think I slept at all that night after having slept so long in the afternoon, but I was grateful just to have a warm, comfortable bed to lie down on. I was content to simply savor the comfort and warmth of the bed and blankets. Whether I slept or not, it didn't matter. I spent most of the night mulling over the events of the last few days. There was much to think about.

The next morning, as I looked out the dining room window, I saw again the cross on the cliff above the barn. I still had a deep desire to go up there and didn't know when, or if, I would ever have another chance. So, before we left, I told Jorn I wanted to try to go up to the cross. I knew it would be difficult because I was still very weak. Even the stairs to the second floor of the guest-house were a challenge for me, but I was determined to at least try to get to the cross if Jorn would allow it. Jorn agreed that it would be a great way to end our time there, and Pastor Tomas enlisted the help of Ramon, the man who had brought my clothes to me, and Christian, the man who Jorn had led to the Lord the night before. They supported me, one on each arm, as we all headed out on our quest for the cross. It was slow going on my very sore frostbitten toes. I also tired very quickly, and we had to stop many times so I could rest. But finally, we made it to the cross. The cross, representing the sacrificed life of Jesus, is everything to us. It's hard to conceive of all it really means, but those two men, carrying me under my arms and leading me to the cross, is the heart of God. It was a beautiful picture of the way we need to come alongside the hurting, weak, and lost ones and lead them to the cross of Christ. I was so grateful for the opportunity they gave me to stand up there beside the cross. There I could take in all the wonder and beauty of that place and say, "God is good!" I can't even begin to put into words all I was feeling inside as I sat up there, gazing at the cross and at the camp below. The wonder of all that had happened and God's goodness were overwhelming. For me, it was a glorious way to end my time at Rio Chico. We had gone up to the cross using the short cut, but I asked them to take me the long way on the way back down!

When we got back to camp, it was time to go. It was hard to say good-bye to these people who had done so much for me. Juan asked me not to allow fear of what happened keep me from coming back. I assured him it would not and that someday, I would be back. With hugs all around and one last wave of the hand, Jorn and I got into one of the trucks and followed Pastor Tomas, Brenda, Gabby, and Christian in the lead truck. We had a six-hour drive ahead of us. It was a precious time of sharing about the week

> **Pastor Ron** – "I finally had a chance to talk to LeAnn when she and Jorn were driving up to Juarez. She didn't talk a whole lot because she was pretty worn out, but I asked about her frostbite, and made sure Jorn was taking good care of her. I also told her how happy everyone was that she was ok and told her I loved her."

as well as a host of other things, but we really didn't talk much about the last few days. It was all still too overwhelming. We had a lot to work through, and it was just too soon. Along the way, we stopped at Gonzalo's house and took time to have tea with him and his wife. I was happy to meet Antonio there. He was one of the trackers who had been looking for any sign of me.

Somewhere along the way Jorn called Pastor Ron and after chatting with him for a few minutes, he handed his phone to me. It was wonderful to have a chance to talk with him. He asked how I was feeling and about my fingers and toes. He assured me they had all been praying fervently for my protection, and everyone was very thankful that God had taken care of me. He brought tears to my eyes when he told me he loved me, and I could say no more.

> **Pastor Ron** – "When they were back in Juarez, I called Jorn again and told him the plans were all set for the Wednesday evening celebration. He told me he still wasn't sure LeAnn would be up to it, but I told him the church really wanted to see her. I told him I would understand if she couldn't make it or if she wanted to stop in just long enough to say "hi." I asked him to talk to her and let me know if she would be up to at least stopping in, but we are going to have the celebration with or without her."

Fearing that if I started to cry I'd never be able to stop, I handed the phone back to Jorn.

Back in Juarez, Brenda arranged for a kind gentleman to take Jorn and me out to do some shopping. Along the way, he stopped the van to pick up a woman and young girl. None of them spoke any English, but Jorn and I did our best to try to communicate with them. It took us quite some time to discover that our "hitchhikers" were the gentleman's daughter and granddaughter, but we had a great time talking and laughing with them. When we got to the market, shop owners were beginning to close their doors, so we didn't have a lot of time, but I managed to find gifts for my nephews and a warm Indian blanket like those we'd had at camp which was a "must have."

After we got back to the Bible Institute we went out to dinner, celebrating Valentine's Day with Pastor Tomas, his wife, Maria, and Brenda. We spent the night again at the Bible Institute.

When I looked up at the cross that morning, I really wanted to be able to go up there. God understood my desire and need to go there. God is with us in giving us the desires of our hearts. Psalm 37:4 says, "Delight yourself in the Lord and He will give you the desires of your heart" (NIV). I don't think that means He will give us everything we think we want, but that He will put His desires for us in our hearts and He delights in fulfilling those desires.

One of many heroes

Ramon & Christian help me get to the cross

Celebration at the cross

Pastor Jorn

Chapter Thirty-Three

GOING HOME

by LeAnn

Very early the next morning, Pastor Tomas, Maria, and Brenda took us back across the border to the airport in El Paso. They dropped Jorn and me off at the curb, and we said our quick good-byes. When Jorn and I finally got settled at the gate to wait for our flight, he told me there was something he had to tell me. Because of the seriousness of his tone, those words scared me more than anything that had happened all weekend! He told me that on Saturday, they decided they needed to file a missing persons report with the authorities and an investigator had come out to camp to ask questions about my disappearance. After getting the preliminary information, the investigator left but said he would be back later with more questions. At that point, Pastor Tomas decided it would be best to take the team back to Juarez because they did not have visas. Jorn told me he called the guys out of the mountains, and they hurriedly packed up so he and Brenda could take them back to Juarez. They had also told the group that if anyone asked what they were doing in Mexico to say they were tourists and not mention anything about being in Rio Chico to do ministry because that requires a different visa which is more restrictive. Of course, I missed out on those instructions and said more than I should have during the radio interview. He told me he nearly panicked when he walked in on the interview. He said there could be serious repercussions for Pastor Tomas and Brenda if the investigator heard my interview on the radio. I was crushed to think that my actions could cause additional trouble for them when I was only trying to let people know about the good work he was doing among the Indians and possibly generate support for his ministry. We prayed fervently that only good would come from my interview.

On the flight from El Paso to Atlanta, Jorn and I were seated next to each other, but after takeoff, he found a few empty seats where he could stretch out and try to catch up on some sleep. I was so overwhelmed with all that had happened, I knew sleep would be impossible for me and as it turned out Jorn

123

Pastor Ron – "Jorn's wife, Bonnie, was planning to drive LeAnn's parents to the Harrisburg airport to meet LeAnn and Jorn. She stopped by the church that afternoon and mentioned that their van was not working properly, and she was going to take it to their mechanic, Davy, who was just back from Mexico himself. I was not about to have anything stand in the way of Jorn and LeAnn getting home safely and in time for our celebration, so I insisted she take my van. I handed her my keys along with some newspaper articles for LeAnn to look at and an email we had received at the church from her friend, Roberto, in Argentina."

wasn't able to sleep either. We both had a lot to deal with. Our minds were filled with so many unanswered questions. I was thinking about all Jorn had told me about how they were searching and screaming when it seemed to me as if no one was out there with me but God. How was it possible that I could hear the dogs and roosters back at camp and not hear their yelling, whistles, and horn blowing? I knew in my heart they'd be out looking for me, but I didn't see or hear any evidence of that and wondered at times if they had abandoned me. I had wondered where they were when they were thinking the same of me.

As soon as our feet hit the ground in Atlanta, we were off and it was all I could do to keep up with Jorn in my weakened state. We both had calls to make and we didn't have a lot of time, so we made them while we walked, practically ran, to our next gate. Jorn wanted me to make an appointment with my medical doctor, so I called my parents and asked them to take care of that. After a few failed attempts, I also reached a friend at work who said he nearly panicked when he thought about the possibility of my not coming back. He was relieved to find out that I was back on American soil, and I asked him to let everyone know that I was okay and would be back to work as soon as I could.

I knew this would probably be my last opportunity to talk to Jorn alone because we wouldn't be seated together on the next flight. I wanted to somehow convey to him my gratefulness for all he had done for me over the last few days; but words just weren't enough, and I began to cry for the first time. People surrounded us there at the gate, but I couldn't stop the tears. I told Jorn I didn't know how I was going to get through seeing my parents and everyone who would be at the church waiting to celebrate our homecoming. I was going to be an emotional wreck. I continued to cry quietly for a few minutes into the flight. My mind was consumed by what was to come after we reached the airport in Harrisburg and arrived back at the church.

Before we knew it, we were at the Harrisburg Airport where we were met by Jorn's wife, Bonnie, and my parents. Mom was prepared with a large box of Kleenex, but we didn't need them. God's grace was carrying us through. We were taken from there directly to our church where there was a huge celebration already in progress. The children poured out of the building into the parking lot as soon as we pulled in, only to run back in and announce to everyone, "She's here; she's here."

I was a bit reluctant to go in, but Pastor Ron came outside, put his arm around me, and led me inside. I had told him earlier in the day that I don't like being the center of attention, but it was wonderful to be surrounded again by the love of so many family members and friends as well as our Grace Covenant family. I was especially anxious to be reunited with the members of our missions team, but I was also happily surprised to see aunts and cousins and my group of friends, aka "The Gang." Jorn and I had endured a very long day and we were both very tired, but the love of God and those around us carried us through the evening.

At the beginning of the service, Pastor Ron asked the missions team to come forward and we did, midst much cheering, clapping, and God praising. Of course he handed me a microphone. My heart was so full, I could hardly speak, but I told

Melody Bratton – "I was praying for LeAnn after I got the call on Saturday morning and I thought, 'She's a worshiper. She stands in front of our church and leads us in worship, into battle.' And it made me realize how important our praise is to the Lord. He's our deliverer and in time of need, where else can we turn, but to Him. On Sunday, Bobby stood up and said that when he heard LeAnn was missing, he wanted to hop on a plane and go down there and save her, but all he could do was fight for her on his knees. God is worthy of praise in every situation and He inhabits the praise of His people. He cares about our every need, whether it is a cut finger or if we're lost in Mexico, relief is in praise. This was such a faith-building event for all of us. We saw God's faithfulness and His power at work. He is all-powerful, and He cared enough about us to bring our team safely home."

Margaret Leddy – "As I was praying for LeAnn, I was standing on Romans 8.:31 which says, 'If God is for us, who can be against us? He who did not spare his own Son, but gave Him up for us all – how will He not also, along with Him, graciously give us all things?' and verses 38 and 39, 'For I am convinced that neither death nor life, neither angels nor demons, neither the present nor the future, nor any powers, neither height nor depth, nor anything else in all creation, will separate us from the love of God that is in Christ our Lord.' I knew that not for one moment, not for a second, was she out of the love of God and He held her in His hands."

them all how much I loved them and thanked them for their concern and prayers. I also thanked God for his protection and provision. I told them I had had no fear throughout my ordeal and was totally confident that I would be rescued. I also told them I was convinced God had worked a miracle in sparing my life.

Jorn was given the opportunity to speak. He echoed my gratefulness for the congregation's prayers and concern. He told them he had never felt such peace in the midst of so much turmoil. He knew it was because these dear ones and so many others were lifting us up before the throne of grace. He said he and I had both experienced the peace that passes all understanding. He too attributed my rescue to a supernatural miracle of God. He said, "If you don't believe in miracles, let me tell you what, you're looking at one tonight!"

We then did what we had come to do and that was to celebrate the goodness of our God. Pastor Ron said, "We've been standing on God's Word, we've been speaking it, proclaiming it, praying it and tonight we are going to reflect on the power of God's word and the power of praise."

Sharon Werner, the worship leader for the evening said it well when she said, "We sought the Lord out of our desperation on LeAnn's behalf. We were the church, the body of Christ, joined together in unity and purpose. He answered our cry. He's our shepherd, our comforter, our refuge and our strength. He guards and He guides. He covers and then He uncovers. He is our help in time of need. He's a warrior, a defender, and our deliverer. He's so faithful. He is the rock of our salvation. He is King of kings and Lord of lords, and there is no God like Him!"

That led into a powerful time of worship followed by testimonies by several members of the congregation. Then Pastor Roberta taught on Psalm 91. She had decided several weeks earlier that she was going to teach on Psalm 91 this very evening. It is so amazing to see how God orchestrates things. He knows the beginning from the end and pulls all the pieces together.

She told the congregation we had seen a demonstration of God's power on Sunday. We were pressed, and we pressed in to God. He brought us hope in the midst of a desperate situation. Psalm 91:1 says, "He who dwells in the shelter of the Most High will rest in the shadow of the Almighty" (NIV). She said she believes that's where I was when I was lost, in the shelter of the Almighty. Verse 4 says, "He will cover you with his feathers" (NIV), and she said the prayers of the people were that covering. She said she was surprised but grateful that I had had no fear. That promise comes in verse 5, "You will not fear the terror of night" (NIV). She said it was my faith in God and the prayers I knew were being said on my behalf, which gave me freedom from fear.

Pastor Roberta also said she believes God's angels were over and around me because verses 11 and 12 tell us, "He will command His angels concerning you, to guard you in all your ways; they will lift you up in their hands, so that you will not strike your foot against a stone" (NIV). You know that I too believe there were angels protecting me, but Pastor Roberta had not yet heard about my very special angels. She closed by saying it's all about God's love and our love for Him. His love is powerful. It casts out fear and takes us into a place of faith. And it's our love for God that puts His power behind our faith and puts it to work.

The service was ended with a couple of my favorite songs. One says, "I fear nothing at all when I'm safe in the arms of my father and if ever I fall, I take comfort in knowing that You are there." For those three days I was in the arms of my Father, and I knew He was going to take care of me, no matter what. The other song was, "How Great Is Our God" and one of its lines says, "All will see, how great is our God." I hope our story helps you to see the greatness of our God and to know His presence and His peace in the midst of your struggles.

Chapter Thirty-Four

UNANSWERED QUESTIONS

by Pastor Jorn

Sam – "God used the events of our trip to grow the faith in each one of us. From day one, we were put to the test in many areas. From the vehicles that needed repairs, to the trip down the mountain, to the rats in the barn and the experience with the electricity, each challenge worked together to build our faith. When I woke up on Saturday morning and saw the ice on the creek, I thought about my hunting experiences and how cold it can get when you are sitting out in the mountains for a couple of hours even with a heavy coat on. I thought about LeAnn and how cold she must be after being out there all night. And if that wasn't bad enough, she wasn't found that day and she was out again a second night. I didn't say anything to anyone else, but I wasn't expecting to find her alive after two nights in the cold. I know that God had to have protected her and her miraculous rescue served to build our faith even more."

During the last flight home, my mind was consumed with thoughts about the things that had happened, and I was trying to come up with some explanation for how it all took place. I (Jorn) thought about the two Tarahumara Indians that had tracked LeAnn for two days, but neither could find a single footprint. I had assumed that where she was found was where she had been the whole time, but on our way back to Juarez, LeAnn told me where she thought she was that first night. She was probably only a mile and a half from camp. I wondered how it could be that there were thirty people out there screaming her name, yet she never heard one voice. While I was talking to God about all these things, I thought to myself, when I get to heaven, reverently I am going to find the Lord and point down and ask, "What was that, what in the world was all that?" because I was, and still am, perplexed by what happened.

The verse that says, what the devil has meant for evil, God will use for good came to my mind; and I was thinking about how much I hate the devil and his schemes. But the more I meditated, I just felt in my spirit that God was in control of everything. I believe there were supernatural things He wanted to do and have happen that were beyond whatever the devil's tricks might have been.

I was reminded of the scripture in Romans 8:28. It says, "And we know that in all things God works for the good of those who love Him, who have been called according to His purpose" (NIV). That was the scripture God really put in my heart as I was thinking about the events that had unfolded during those days we were together in Mexico and especially during the last three days when LeAnn was lost. I believe God had a specific plan and purpose, and He needed to use someone to get things done in people's hearts in Mexico and even in our church back in Lewistown.

This whole experience caused some things to happen

LeAnn – Weeks later God was still using this experience to bring people together. One Saturday morning, my aunt and uncle who were spending the winter in Florida went out for breakfast. On their way home they noticed a yard sale. They normally avoid stopping along this particularly busy stretch of highway, but that morning, they stopped to take a look. While my aunt was browsing she overheard a conversation between two women standing nearby. One woman was telling the other about her brother-in-law who had been on a missions trip in Mexico when one of the team members had gotten lost. She spoke of how he and the others went out searching for the one who was lost. My aunt had to know if this was the same missions trip that I had been on. She interrupted the conversation and asked how long ago this had taken place. When the woman said it had been a few weeks ago, my aunt exclaimed, "That was my niece!" Of course they hugged, cried, and laughed together, amazed that they had stopped at the yard sale and had been there just as Shawn's sister-in-law was relating our story to a friend. It was an encounter only God could have orchestrated.

in peoples' lives, the kind of things that help you to really believe and trust God in a special and unique way for your life. This experience was not just about LeAnn needing to have hope in Christ, knowing that whatever happened, she was in God's hands. But the fact is that God was moving in the lives of everyone there. When you look at the team of individuals that went to Rio Chico, where they are relationally with each other, and what God had done to knit their hearts together, you begin to understand the importance of having an eternal perspective. The more we can see beyond our natural circumstances, the more we begin to look at things from God's perspective and understand His plan and purpose in our lives. Everything, no matter how small we think the circumstance is, has a ripple effect that grows as it moves outward. God took this one event and used it for multiple purposes.

Much of it involved relationships. He solidified the relationship between Ron and me. He did something relationally between us as pastors and the church. He also did something relationally between my team and me, and He built trust into the relationship between Tomas and Brenda and me. He brought all those different Mexican groups who had never worked together before, into relationship over a lost gringo. Why would they care about this American over any other American? Lots of Americans have been down there, but it was God who brought them together and put concern in their hearts for LeAnn.

He also taught us all lessons about our character, our nature, and the things in our lives that needed to change. He did all those things, many things through one event. Tragedy, crisis, con-

> **Pastor Ron** – "Several people have mentioned to me that our crisis in Mexico was sort of like George Bush's twin towers. He was new to his office when the terrorists attacked, and I had only been ordained a couple of weeks before this happened. I believe this event was much more significant than just what it meant to LeAnn's life. There were a lot of things God was doing in many different people through this experience. I've often asked the question, why was this so significant? We've scratched the service, but I don't think we've fully tapped into all that God has done in people's hearts and lives. I will never forget what happened and most people won't. I believe it's important that we are reminded occasionally of the miracle God worked on our behalf."

130

flict, pressure, whatever you want to call it—He did multiple things through one event because God is eternal, and He has an eternal plan. When I begin to look into eternity, it helps me to understand how God gathers people together and what God is doing supernaturally in people's lives. My conclusion is that it's all about relationship.

God knew what was ahead of us in Mexico long before we left. I believe He prepared me in advance for the things that happened. I also believe the trip and the crisis that played out in Mexico were very important to where we were as a church at the time. It solidified the leadership roles Ron and I carried now that Michael had just officially stepped down. It also solidified our positions of authority. Because I had Christ's power of authority and the authority given me by the church, I was able to speak into people's lives and to know confidently that I didn't have to wring my hands and worry about things, but instead, I was able to make tough decisions in a crisis situation. I believe that was all part of the process as the events of the week played out.

For myself, there are probably two things I learned. The first one has to do with having confidence in my authority and out of that authority, to make right decisions, though they may be difficult. I think God showed me that I have the ability to find the strength required to make tough decisions when dealing with people. The second thing relates to the scripture that makes the declaration that death no longer has a hold on us. It's not so much about not being afraid of the dying process, but instead, it's being able to say, I'm not afraid of death and what death means or how death affects certain situations.

Another thing I realized out of this experience is that when you really have a heart for people, when caring about people is part of who you are, and it's not just something you do because you think it's expected, then God does something supernatural with every event. When you have that kind of heart for people and they really know you care about their lives, then something substantial and sustaining happens in those relationships. Those who went with me to Mexico know I genuinely cared about them, and because of that, something happened in those relationships that has connected us in a very special way. I believe I will have an eternal connection with those God specifically spoke to me about inviting to come on the trip. With those I knew God wanted there, those I fasted and prayed for, I will have a connection forever.

One of those is Davy Kerstetter. I'm so glad God changed his heart to come along on the trip. Looking back now I realize there is a lot more to Davy than meets the eye, especially in regard to his gifting and his humor. He really has a commitment to the things of God. He's committed to the things that are burning in his heart. It was good to see God use him that way when we were on the trip, to see him relaxed and enjoying what he was doing. Though he was serious at times, he was very encouraging as well. Had he not gone, the trip still would have been fun, but he just pushed everything over the edge with his humor, and it wouldn't have been the same without him.

I also see the importance of seeing a person for who they are, valuing them, and understanding that God is so in love with them. When I do that, I can love them the way God loves them and care about their whole personhood, their personalities and quirks, everything about them that makes them different and unique. They don't have to be just like me in order for me to love them and that's part of being able to feel the heart of God for people. There's nothing like the kind of spiritual, emotional, and physical struggles that we experienced to help you to see and help people in the right way, to love them the way God loves them. It was because I loved my team and cared about what they were going through that I could tell them they were not going across the border. They were able to accept my decision because they knew there was real love behind it.

We have to be committed to people. We can't demand loyalty from someone, waiting for proof they love you before you return love to them. It's about being willing to love others and be loyal to them even though they've not yet shown love or proved their loyalty to you. But that's exactly what God did for us through Christ. He loved us when we had not yet chosen to love Him. So when you do that—love first—something supernatural happens in our relationships. It doesn't happen every time, we still get hurt sometimes and relationships don't always work out; but it's the heart of God that we love unconditionally, and that's where we really learn how to care about people. That truth was driven home to me through our experience. For me, that was very significant, and I realize that is the kind of love I want to give to people every day of my life.

My relationship with Pastor Tomas and Brenda went to another level when we went through this crisis together. Our relationships had been strengthening over the last couple of years, but when LeAnn was lost, it gave them an opportunity to see our character. They were able to watch our reaction to adversity and see us handle it in a proper way. We didn't blame anyone. We trusted God. I think that spoke to them about who we are. Now, he trusts me and knows I genuinely care about his ministry and his family, and that I want to serve him in his ministry. There is a level of trust now we didn't have before. It was a powerful test for our relationship. How would we respond to him and how would he respond to us during the crisis? It strengthened our relationship because he was able to see that we were faithful and not going to give up. When something like this happens, some might say, "I'm never coming back here again, you didn't tell me enough information; you could have explained better how to get to the cross, why didn't you have signs posted?" There were a lot of accusations that could have been brought and blamed on him or his ministry, but we never did that. Our response during the crisis strengthened our relationship for the future and also said a lot about the people I had brought with me.

A week after we returned, I was in a pastor's meeting with Michael and Wes and Ron. They said, "Well, Jorn, what did you learn from that trip?" I said, "I learned a couple of things: number one is that no matter where we are in the world, no one will ever go anywhere alone again, no matter what. Number two is that we are going to paint signs showing the way to that cross!"

Chapter Thirty-Five

GOD OF MIRACLES

by Pastor Tomas

When I (Tomas) think of LeAnn's experience in the wilderness, like Jorn, I think of her as the lost sheep Jesus spoke about in His parable of the lost sheep in Luke 15.

I don't believe everything that happened to LeAnn was an accident. I believe God had taken one of His sheep and tucked her away in the mountains for a divine purpose, to teach us something about how He feels toward the lost. When we realized LeAnn was lost, we immediately began our desperate search. And when our search stretched throughout the night into the next day and again into the night, our urgency to find her grew. We knew we needed to find her before it was too late. We wouldn't stop looking until she was found. But as we searched, God was allowing us to catch a glimpse of His heart for the lost. Because LeAnn was lost, we now have a better understanding of how God feels about the many thousands of Indians who are lost in the Copper Canyon. Sometimes, we make plans for what we will do the next year, but we are not always conscious of the urgency of their need. Those people are sick, in need of healing. They are

Brenda – "I believe that what happened was part of God's plan. If the enemy were behind it, he would have taken LeAnn's life. He comes to steal, kill, and destroy and he had every opportunity to destroy her life. I believe God had something prepared for LeAnn and for others as well. It was a great example to all of us of God's protection. It seems incredible to me when I look at the cross in front of camp and realize that LeAnn got lost on her way there, even though it is in plain sight. Isn't that what happens so often though? Many people miss God's love even when it is right in front of them."

Larry – "If I had to sum up our whole experience in one word, that word would be 'miraculous.' Before we left on the trip Pastor Jorn talked to us about Pastor Tomas and he said, 'You're not going to believe this, but that man lives from miracle to miracle'. At the time I thought that was really neat, but I didn't really understand the depth of what he was saying until I was down there for a full week and experienced it for myself. Let me tell you, that man lives from miracle to miracle. And somehow we were thrown into this miraulous realm that he lives in and were blessed to experience it for ourselves. There were a lot of supernatural things happening daily that if you try to wrap your human mind around them, you can't really give an explanation. It was just miraculous, and we knew it was the hand of God. It wasn't us because we were limited in what we could do, but when we reached the point of our limitation, that's when God took over and He did the rest. At the end of the day we would talk about the different things that happened and were amazed by what God had done. Our only conclusion was that God is just so good. John 20:30 says, "Jesus did many other miraculous signs in the presence of his disciples" and we think he was talking about His disciples 2000 years ago and I think he was, but I think he was also talking about the 12 disciples that went to Mexico, because in our presence, He did many miraculous things" (NIV).

hungry and need somebody to feed them. They are lost and very cold because they have nothing to cover themselves. They live out their lives in the same way LeAnn lived for those three days. But unlike LeAnn, many die, without ever knowing of the love God has for them.

The Lord did not forget LeAnn when she was lost. He had His mighty hand upon her. We had many questions concerning her whereabouts, but He knew exactly where she was the whole time she was away from us. The Lord said, "I'm going to do a mighty work here." I believe this is why He allowed the situation to happen in the first place. He did do a mighty work, a work that will continue. I believe that because LeAnn was lost and later found, many more of the lost sheep will be found and brought into the warm and loving arms of our Lord. I know the Lord gave her strength. He was with her and He took care of her. He performed a miracle on her behalf. In the minds of many people, she had already died, but the Lord raised her from the dead. Just as He did with Jesus who died on Friday and was raised to life on Sunday, she was close to death, but the Lord gave her life back to her that glorious Sunday afternoon.

We need to realize that the Lord is teaching us something deeper out of this experience. What happened that weekend was not normal or natural; it was supernatural. God was trying to get our attention and to teach us things close to His heart. I know God has many things to teach LeAnn out of her being lost and found, dead and now raised to new life. As she seeks God, He will reveal those things to her, but we all need to seek the Lord and ask Him what it is He wants us to learn from this experience. These things that happened had a huge impact in the hearts and lives of the residents of Rio Chico and the surrounding towns and villages. It brought people, who otherwise might never have met, together to celebrate the goodness of God.

Larry rescuing Denny from certain death

Chapter Thirty-Six

THE MASTER PLAN

by LeAnn

I am convinced that God had a plan and a purpose for my being lost. The team was so close to where I spent the first night in the wilderness that I should have been found; but no matter what they or I did, I would not be found until God's purpose was accomplished. I am certain that a part of His purpose was for Christian to have the opportunity to give his heart to the Lord. Jorn mentioned changed relationships and Pastor Ron speaks about the faith that rose up in all of us, and there may be other reasons that have not yet been revealed to us. I do know that God is faithful, and He had me wrapped in His warm and loving arms. I know that it's only by His grace I am saved! And in that, God is glorified. As Jorn told the team that Saturday night, in every situation of our lives we have the opportunity to glorify God and this was certainly one of them.

As I have reflected on what happened in Mexico, it has occurred to me and to others that this experience happened just a short time after the leadership change at Grace Covenant Church took place. Pastor Ron had been made pastor and Jorn had been made associate pastor just days before our mission trip began. Yet both Ron and Jorn rose to the challenges that the crisis presented. Ron led the congregation with power and confidence. At the Sunday morning worship service he encouraged his people by claiming victory. The praise and worship service was powerful, and his words were words of strength and courage. In Mexico, though concerned for my safety, Jorn stepped aside and allowed Pastor Tomas to lead the search while he did all he could to aid that effort and support and encourage the rest of the team. He did not let the circumstance shake him from his work. He could have easily decided to rest after I was found, but he remained determined to win another soul for Jesus. Jorn spent time in deep prayer to receive the word of knowledge from the Lord about Christian's life. Then he took the time to share the word with Christian and led him, a lost soul, to the cross of Christ. He did that gently and lovingly, much like Christian led me to the cross that stands high above the Rio Chico. The Lord's work continued despite it all.

Since my safe return home, I have had a lot of time to reflect on the experience. It is abundantly clear to me how each of the daily devotion times provided nuggets of truth that not only were important to our team, but they all can be applied in our daily walk with the Lord.

I remember Jorn's question about fear. His question certainly had a prophetic element. Looking back now, I realize that when Diane and I had gone up the mountain with the children, we had been nervous, fearing one of them might get hurt. Yet none of us had ever expressed a concern about being lost. I recall Shawn's story about running with the Mexican men in response to the sound of distress that turned out to be a goat being attacked by a wild dog. I was protected from those thoughts while I was lost. Had I begun to dwell on the idea of wild animals stalking me in the dark, my faith may have rapidly eroded into sheer panic. Instead, I felt God's presence.

I have also thought about another of Jorn's teachings from that week, from Psalm 37:7. We are to sit in expectation of what God is going to do in our lives. We sometimes miss it because He moves gently. When we don't wait on Him, we are in the flesh and He cannot be glorified in it. I realize that while I was lost I did react in my own flesh and left my place by the river despite repeatedly hearing the Lord telling me to be still. I knew in my heart that when lost, one should stay still; but out of desperation and impatience, I chose to go back up on the mountain.

Recently I was remembering again the night before I got lost when Pastor Tomas shared with us, and I thought about the way I had wept; uncontrollable tears welled up from deep inside my spirit. As I was thinking about that, I was reminded of Jesus' agony in the garden the night before His crucifixion. I wondered if there was something God wanted me to understand about what was happening that evening. Was there something about that night in the garden that prepared our Lord for what was ahead? Was there a connection between what I experienced that evening in the dining room and what I was to experience the next day? I decided to read the account of Jesus in the garden in each of the gospels. The first gospel I looked at was Luke and indeed, there was something there I had not noticed before. After Jesus prayed, "Yet not my will, but yours be done," God's Word says, "At once an angel from heaven was at his side, strengthening him." Was that what God wanted to show me? Was the Holy Spirit at work in me that night, giving me strength to cope with the ordeal ahead? I believe it's very possible He was.

Then, I remember the words from James 2:4, to "Consider it a sheer gift when tests and challenges come to you from all sides." We are not to try to get out of it prematurely. Sometimes we go through wilderness experiences to teach us something about ourselves and/or something about God. It can also be a time of preparation where we are molded and shaped, conformed into the image and likeness of Jesus.

On the one-year anniversary of my being lost, Pastor Ron preached a message entitled, "The Wilderness Test." He said the wilderness is a place of "divine development." First Peter 3:6-7 say, "Pure gold, put in the fire comes out *proved pure*, genuine faith put through this suffering comes out *proved genuine*. When Jesus wraps this all up, it's your faith, not your gold that God will have on display as evidence of his victory." We saw that happen. Our faith was tested in this experience, and it was proved genuine. It was our faith in God that brought the victory over our situation.

> **Shawn** – "I believe God used this whole experience to bring our whole team closer together. Our worship that Sunday morning when we were praying for LeAnn was powerful. We and everyone else had done all we could do in our own strength, but then we saw God take over and bring our crisis to a victorious conclusion."

He also said, "Only by dependence, will we reach deliverance." I believe God may have been waiting for each of us, Pastor Jorn, Pastor Ron, and me, to come to that place of complete and utter dependence. For all of us, it happened on Sunday afternoon. For me it happened there by the river, for Jorn it was on a rock next to the path that led back up to the truck, and for Ron it was in his bedroom. We were all, at practically the same time, crying out to God because we knew there was nothing more we could do. He was our only hope, and out of our dependence on Him, we found deliverance.

Pastor Ron said that God uses difficult times to teach us things He wants us to know about ourselves. I have learned that I am a stronger person than I thought I was—physically, emotionally, and spiritually. Jorn told me he was surprised I was not crying when he met

> **Diane** – "It was a week of many miracles; amazing things, and you know, LeAnn's being lost and found was just the grand finale of all the things that had happened during our time in Mexico."

me in the ambulance. Others have asked if I cried when I was out there, and I did a little, but probably for less than a minute and then only because I thought I should be upset. It seemed somehow abnormal not to be upset by the situation I was in, but I wasn't. It was as if a strength and resolve rose up inside of me that I did not know was there. It was the peace of God and the assurance that He was with me and would rescue me.

After I was rescued, I carefully guarded my emotions. I felt that if I started to cry, I would never be able to stop. Looking back on the experience has opened my eyes to what could have happened. The thought of all the things that could have gone wrong while I was out there became evident. I could have been injured when I fell. I could have encountered a mountain lion or a frightened wild dog. About a week after we got home, Jorn told me to write down what I was planning to share at our church. I believe he also realized that I wasn't dealing with my emotions, and he knew that writing about what had happened would begin the healing process for me. It was then that I started allowing myself to cry but still only for short periods of time. I could not really deal with it all at once, but writing our story has brought a lot of healing to those emotions. Being able to see God's hand in this and to see His goodness and grace at work in my life, in my family, in my fellow team members, and in our church has made it easier to look back and to share the story with others.

Several years ago, during one of our Life Group meetings, Pastor Jorn had a prophetic word for me. He said as he was praying for me, he saw a buttercup, a wildflower that grows up new in the spring of each year. He said he believed God was going to do something in the springtime that would bring me a newness of life. Of course, I got ahead of God again and assumed He meant the next spring. Nothing significant happened that spring, but I never forgot that word. I even picked a buttercup to keep in my Bible and dug up some along a country road to plant next to my house as a reminder of that promise from God. I now believe that word was referring to what would happen on our missions trip to Mexico.

God heard my cry on Tuesday morning when I asked Him to use my life for His glory and He knew my desire to come back from there more in love with Him. Hosea 2:14-15 says,

And now, here's what I'm going to do. I'm going to start all over again. I'm taking her out into the wilderness where we had our first date, and I'll court her. I'll give her bouquets of roses. I'll turn Heartbreak Valley into Acres of Hope. She'll respond like she did as a young girl, those days when she was fresh out of Egypt.

Some might think that the enemy led me out there, but I don't believe that. God felt so close that afternoon as I walked up over the mountain and shared my wonder with Him at the beauty all around me. And He gave me hope in my desperate situation. In a canyon that could have been filled with hopelessness and despair, He filled me with a childlike faith and peace. In verse 18, it says, "At the same time I'll make a peace treaty between you and the wild animals and birds and reptiles and get rid of all weapons of war. Think of it! Safe from beasts and bullies!" He did that too. He kept me safe from any number of things that could have harmed me while I was in that wilderness.

Verses 19-20 say, "And then I'll marry you for good—forever! I'll marry you true and proper, in love and tenderness. Yes, I'll marry you and neither leave you nor let you go. You'll know me, God, for who I really am." These verses speak of marriage to God, a relationship more intimate that any other, and He promises that kind of relationship with us—one He promises never to break. It's in the wilderness experiences of life that our intimacy with God grows deeper, and we learn to know Him for who He really is.

Later on in Hosea 6:1-3, it says,

Come, let us return to the Lord. He has torn us to pieces, but he will heal us, he has injured us, but he will bind up our wounds. After two days he will revive us; on the third day he will restore us, that we may live in his presence. Let us acknowledge the Lord; let us press on to acknowledge him. As surely as the sun rises, he will appear; he will come to us like the winter rains, like the spring rains that water the earth.

I believe He took me to the wilderness. I had to endure those long cold nights and those days spent alone in that place so I could know His power and His love for me. And as Jorn said, on the third day, like it also says in this scripture, I was restored so that I could know Him more and live more fully in His presence. Praise God! And like the buttercup that springs to life after the spring rains come to water the earth, so too my life has been renewed and I lift my face to bask in the sunshine of His love. To go back again to Hosea 14:5 it says, "I will make a fresh start with Israel. He'll burst into bloom like a crocus in the spring."

I expected this trip to be "life changing," but I had no idea what God had in store for me. One of the things that Jorn said when we shared the story with our church was that on that Friday I had literally gone into the grave; but, oh, for Sunday, when I came out! It is like that, as if I have been reborn. I am not the same person that walked away from camp that Friday afternoon. My whole focus has changed.

One of the reasons that I put on my application for coming on this trip was so that I would become more "others minded," and I believe I've grown in that. Second Corinthians 7:11-13 says,

> *Isn't it wonderful all the ways in which this distress has goaded you closer to God? You're more alive, more concerned, more sensitive, more reverent, more human, more passionate, more responsible. Looked at from any angle, you've come out of this with purity of heart.*

God used this experience to change my heart in a number of ways. He has made me more alive, with a newly defined purpose. I believe I am more concerned, sensitive, passionate, and compassionate, especially to the needs of the Tarahumara Indians. My friends at Rio Chico and the Tarahumara Indians are never far from my thoughts. One morning when I went for a walk along the river at Rio Chico, I picked up a stone thinking that I wanted to take a piece of that place along home with me, but I would not have needed the stone. I think I will always carry a little bit of Rio Chico in my heart, and I've probably left a part of my heart there as well.

Shortly after my return home, I began to realize that as a result of my experience, I had, in some small way, experienced the life of the Tarahumara

Chabela and me

Indians. I spent just two days and two nights out there in the cold with no food or shelter, but the Indians endure long winters in much the same way, with little shelter and not enough food to nourish their bodies properly. Because of that, many of their infants and children die of exposure and starvation, and many of them are doing it all without knowing the love of God. I can't imagine having to try to survive out there without Him.

When I think of precious little Chabela who was brought out of the canyon when she was only two and her brother, Lazaro, who was four at the time, I know there are thousands more children like them back in the canyon who desperately need God and the ministry provided by Pastor Tomas and Brenda. What an honor it was to support them in their ministry to those that have never heard the gospel and who are in such desperate need. I know that we touch the heart of God when we reach out to His lost sheep.

When I think back on the ordeal now, I can clearly see that God never lost sight of me, never let go of me, and never failed me. He had allowed me to be lost for a greater purpose—His purpose! I also believe I have a deeper reverence for God and a deeper revelation of His sovereignty and His love for me. I can only be grateful for His love for me and for all His people. I am also grateful beyond words to all the people who were praying for me. I know those prayers were as vital to my rescue as the men who found me and carried me to safety. Those prayers were carrying me through the ordeal just as surely as those men who carried me out of the canyon.

I'm sure if you asked Larry if the trip were worth it while he was in the midst of his airsickness, he might have hesitated; but, if you ask Larry today if it was worth it, he'll emphatically tell you that, yes, absolutely, it was worth it. I would have to wholeheartedly agree. It was all worth it. Knowing that Christian will spend eternity in heaven with us is worth it. Having an opportunity to continue to bless Pastor Tomas' ministry by sharing my story is worth it. Knowing that God will use this story to bless your life is worth it too. I hope this story of God's faithfulness will deepen your faith and show you how wide, and how high, and how deep is His love for you.

Not only that, but I hope our story will give you a deeper awareness of God's presence with us. Our sin separated us from a holy God, but Jesus' sacrificial death on the cross and the power of His resurrection reconcile us to the Father. It's what brings us into relationship with the Father, Son, and Holy Spirit and allows us to come into and live in His presence. That cross high on the cliff at Rio Chico represents the cross of Christ, the pathway to God's presence. If you haven't walked that path, the one that leads to the Father, by way of the cross, won't you do that now? He's searching for you and He loves you so much. Confess your sin to the Father and accept the free gift of salvation by the blood of His precious Lamb. Jesus, our rescuer! Allow Him to take you by the hand and lead you into the presence of our loving Father.

Epilogue

THE RETURN TRIP

August 2007

Remember that church where the team was worshiping when they heard of my rescue? I found myself there eighteen months to the moment later! The same church building, at the same 5:00 pm Sunday service with those who had been supporting our team and praying along with them for my safe return. My return trip to Mexico had been rescheduled several times, and it wasn't until just days before we were to leave that I realized it would be the eighteen month anniversary of my being lost. I had very much wanted to be there on the one-year anniversary, and that hadn't worked out, but God had arranged this trip to fall over this anniversary without our even realizing it. I was overwhelmed with gratefulness for the opportunity to thank these wonderful people for their love and prayers. They, in turn, were encouraged in their faith to see the answer to their prayers first hand. I was also excited to see two of the little girls we had played with at the Bible Institute the last time we were there.

Juarez was very hot, and I couldn't wait to get to the mountains of Rio Chico where we found the temperatures much more pleasant. Most of all, I was anxious to see the friends we had left behind. The first to greet me was Chabela, who even at five years old seemed to realize how important it was for me to have a shoulder to cry on at that moment. Then there was her mother, Rosenda. We don't seem to need words to communicate the love we feel in our hearts. I found Ramon shoeing a horse in another part of the yard where the boys, Gilberto, Luis, and Lazaro were keeping him company. I was happy to find Gabby there too as he had moved from Juarez to Rio Chico to help on the farm. I was surprised also to find out that he is father to a daughter, Brenda, who is fifteen and a son, David, who is ten. And of course the ever present, Chico or Francisco, but sadly, Juan was no longer there.

Rio Chico's population had grown quite a bit, and there were still more friends to be made. There was the young Indian couple Carlos and Virginia who live a couple of miles up the road at the farm. I was told that Virginia is fifteen years old and has already been married for two years. Her husband is a bit older. They work very hard tending the animals and crops. They made their home in one room of a concrete block building. Everything they owned was contained in that room: their bed, shelves for their clothing, a cupboard, a table, a tiny woodstove, and a couple of chairs. The woods had been their bathroom, but we were there to build one for them, complete with shower, sink, and toilet. And while we were at it, we would paint the inside of their home and build them a front porch. The three men with me and I wouldn't do this alone though. A group from Canada was spending the week with us—still more friends to get to know and work alongside.

There were a lot of things I wanted to do while there. One of those things was to be able to thank the Mexican people for their love and prayers; but the other things involved leaving camp, and I had promised not to do that alone. I ventured as far as the barn and the creek one afternoon, but when I went out later, I found all the gates had been closed around the yard. It seemed as though I was being confined to camp, but I'm sure it was so the horse that was grazing there wouldn't get out. Pastor Jorn had brought another group that week and took my potential guides along with him to the canyon, so I had to lay aside my desire to go back to those places where I had been when I was lost, at least for the time being. The needs around me seemed more important at the time anyway. Virginia and Carlos needed a bathroom more than I needed to see those places. I knew this trip was not about what I wanted to do, but what God wanted to do through me.

The guys took a morning off work to do some hiking with me though, and it was great. We went up to the cross and I nearly lost my breakfast when Ben showed me the ledge Pastor Tomas had gone out on when they were searching for me. It literally made me sick with fear to think of the risk he had taken in going out there to look into the crevasses on either side of the cross. I am so very grateful for God's protection

The ledge

over him and everyone else who scouring those rugged mountains for me.

We then climbed the mountain behind the cross, searching for anything familiar. My only fear in returning to Mexico was being in the mountains in the summertime when we might encounter snakes. I had prayed for months that we wouldn't see any, but sure enough, we did. We encountered a rattlesnake that could have caused a real problem if it had bitten one of us as we were far from camp, but the enemy has to flee at the name of Jesus and he did. We found a trail that I thought I might have been on while I was lost, but we came back with more questions than answers. One of the questions was how I could have found my way down off that mountain in the dark without killing myself. We searched in vain for a way down off the mountain to the river but found none and had to return to camp the way we had come.

I had a drawing with me that my mother had done as I described the place where I was that Friday night and Saturday, eighteen months earlier. I showed it to Ramon one evening, and he seemed to know where it was. He asked me to stay where I was and he returned a little later with another new friend, David, who spoke a little English. With David's help he told me he had been there that Friday night. He had tied his horse at the top of the mountain and walked down the ridge toward the river. He told me he was screaming the whole time and if this is the same place, he would have been just across the river from me on the opposite bank. Ramon was leaving the next morning with Jorn, so he wasn't able to take me out there to verify that it was the same location, but maybe next time.

God has given me a heart for the Tarahumara Indians and the people of Mexico, so when I wasn't working, I was interceding for them and their country. When I was there the last time, I asked God to spare my life. This time I was asking Him to spare the lives of the Indian children, many of whom die before the age of ten, and to bring salvation to the spiritually lost of that land. I also was thinking about the Mexican miners who had lost their lives in Utah just weeks before our trip and asked God to bring prosperity to the country of Mexico so that their people would not need to come to the US to find jobs to support their families back home. Psalm 72:12-14, in speaking of the ruler of the land, says, "For he will deliver the needy who cry out, the afflicted, who have no one to help. He will take pity on the weak and the needy and save the needy ones from death. He will rescue them from oppression and violence, for precious is their blood in his sight" (NIV). It's my prayer that the Mexican leadership would have a change of heart and no longer consider the Indians a burden, a problem that will go away with their extinction, but as lives precious in God's sight and a treasure worth saving.

Afterword

THE "WHYS"

by LeAnn

Our story began with the answers to several questions of why, but it ends with even bigger unanswered questions. *Why did this happen? Why wasn't I found more quickly? Why didn't the others hear my cries for help and why didn't I hear them calling my name? Where was I in relation to where they were looking?*

What do we do with those unanswered questions of why? What do we do when life situations just don't make sense? Do we frantically pursue answers to those questions, trying to find explanations or figure it all out?

I tend to want to do that. I think it is part of our wanting to be in control. But I believe God would have us leave those questions of why at His feet, trusting that He knows the answers to those questions and that's all that matters. We need to relinquish our need to be in control to the One who is in control of all things. God is sovereign and we negate that sovereignty when we insist on asking why. Really, who are we to question God's purposes? It's a bit like when we as children asked why of our parents. They often responded with "because I said so." I think those words were sometimes spoken because our parents didn't really have a good reason or we were too immature to understand why. But everything God does has purpose—purposes that we as His children may not be able to see or comprehend.

Honestly, I struggle with those questions. I want to figure it all out and tie up all the loose ends to our story. I hope He will continue to reveal some of the answers to those questions in His time or when I go back to Rio Chico, but He may also have a reason for not answering those questions just yet. It could be that He may want all of us to learn to let go of the whys, relinquish control and find rest, trusting in His sovereignty. He was there and in control through every moment of our crisis in Mexico, and I believe He will continue to give us glimpses into His plans and purposes not only concerning our story, but for our lives ahead. All glory belongs to Him who knows the beginning from the end!

NOTE TO READERS
FROM PASTOR JORN

Have you ever been lost or lost someone? I've had the privilege of experiencing both. Though I would not wish either on anyone else, the reason I call it a privilege is because of the valuable lessons I learned in the midst of these struggles. It's been over two years since LeAnn was lost; the events that took place over those three days are still very vivid in my mind and spirit. I'm not sure of all the ramifications that were involved in God's plan of redemption in bringing LeAnn back to us but I'm sure of one thing: God in his infinite wisdom and love has his eye on us and lost is only a hopeless situation when He is not involved.

Now reflecting back, I can see that He was with LeAnn and me through the entire process. Though she was lost, I felt just as lost, having nowhere to turn and no answers in why and how LeAnn could slip away from us so easily. There were times when my heart ached knowing that I had no way to help her, as my mind raced through all the ugly scenarios and the possible outcome. I can clearly recall the last day as I sat by myself for a few minutes in frustration after a long walk to the bottom of the canyon and then back up again in search of evidence that LeAnn was still alive. As I sat there running out of time on that third day, I couldn't understand why LeAnn would not have heard us call out her name the thousands of times before. I was tired and at my wits end when I began to cry out the name of Jesus in desperation, hoping that maybe my God would find her. Little did I know that at the same time I was yelling out the name of Jesus and listening to it echo over those canyons, she had been found. I rejoice knowing that in the heart of God, LeAnn and I were never lost, just on a journey to learn more about His love, grace and mercy. Jesus, tender of the lost sheep!

Rejoice, O church of God
I need not tell you to do this
For the lost is found
The fears are quelled
The tears are stopped
And the hearts rejoice
Faithful One, O God
You are faithful
No matter how the story ends
You are faithful
But for this answer to our plea, we thank You!
We honor You for who You are
But we thank You for the answer
The lost is found
The Shepherd cares, watches, carries
Always—His eye is upon us
And we thank Him
Your eye is upon us and we thank You
Thank You, Thank You

—Verna Clemmer, February 12, 2006
(Her heart's response when LeAnn was found in Mexico)